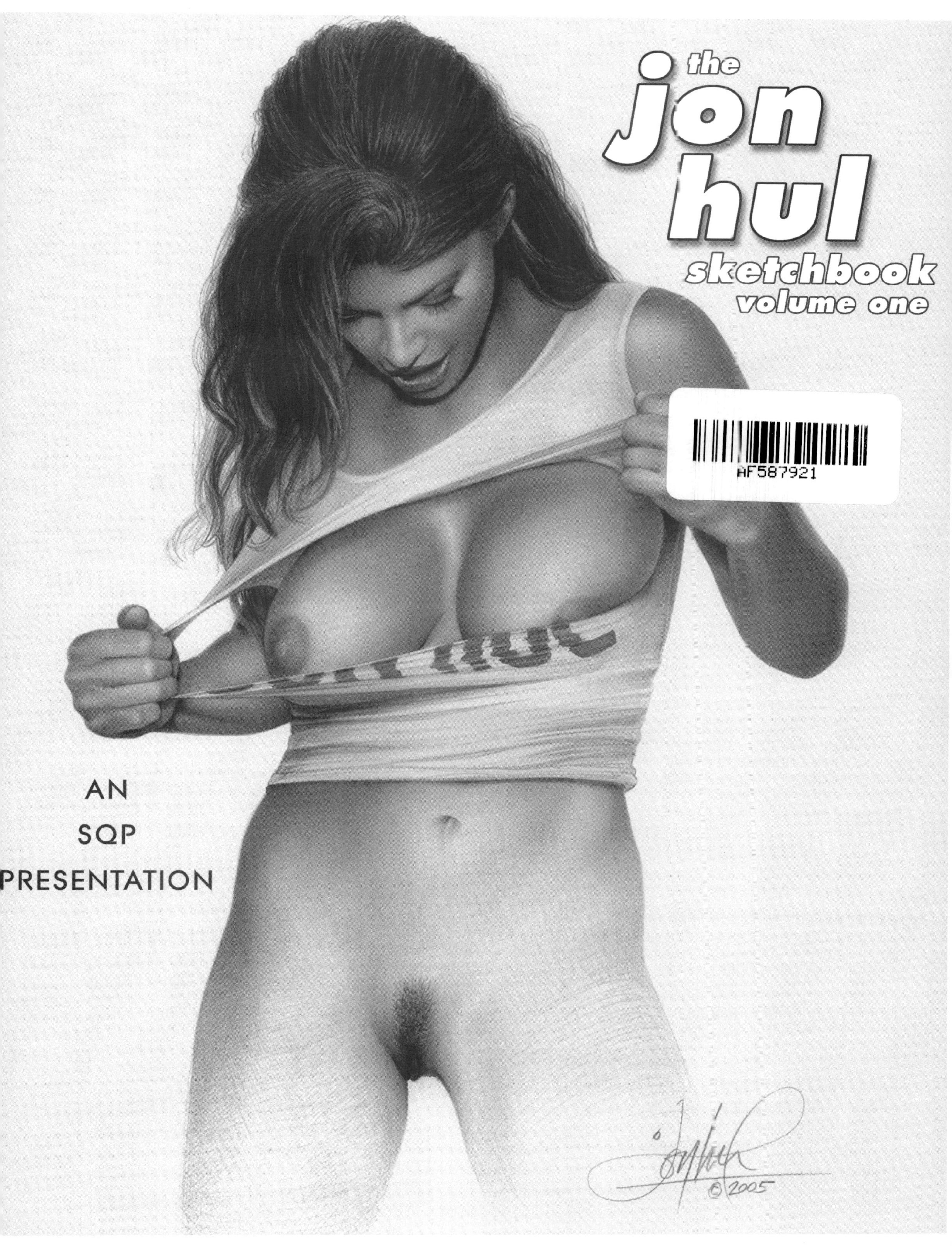
the
jon
hul
sketchbook
volume one
AN
SQP
PRESENTATION
© 2005

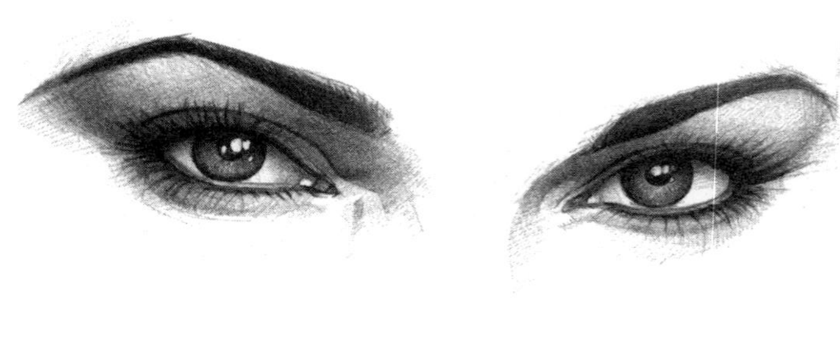

ACKNOWLEDGEMENTS:
JON HUL WANTS TO THANK HIS FAMILY, FRIENDS, AND ASSOCIATES FOR THEIR BELIEF AND SUPPORT: TERINA AND SOFIA HUL, TIFFANY, COBY AND NATHAN ROBINSON, TAMARA AND ROBERT BANE, ANNE SHIRER, MARICEL HIDALGO AND THE ENTIRE BANE STAFF, DEVIN DEVASQUEZ, BARBARA MOORE, ANGELA MIELINI, SUZI SIMPSON, TAILOR JAMES, DESTINY DAVIS, KIM CROSBY, ARIA GIOVANNI, KIRIN AND VICTOR WHITMILL, EMMIT "ICEBERG" GATES, DANNY ROBERTS, AND KAREN AND EMILE REGGIE, BOB SCHULTZ AND MARYANN DOE, AND CONNIE AND SHELDON KASTEN.

A VERY SPECIAL THANK YOU TO:
SAL QUARTUCCIO AND BOB KEENAN AT SQP.

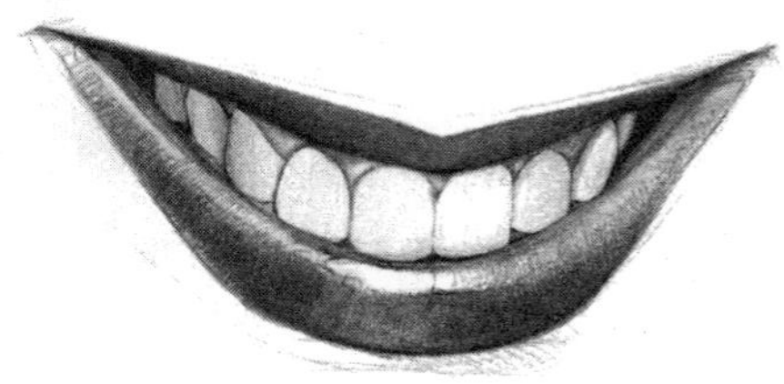

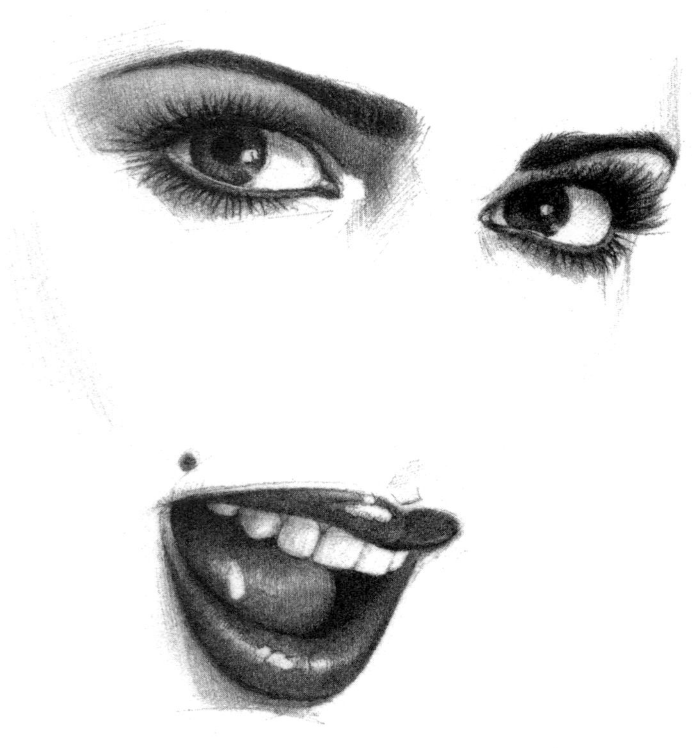

CREDITS:
SOFIA HUL (PHOTOGRAPHY) AND
TIFFANY M. HUL-ROBINSON (POEM)

ART AND LAYOUT:
JON HUL/PIECE OF MIND PRODUCTIONS,
LAS VEGAS, NEVADA, 2006
WWW.JONHULFINEART.COM

THE JON HUL SKETCHBOOK

Volume One

Published by
SQP Inc.
PO Box 248 - Columbus, NJ 08022

Sal Quartuccio & Bob Keenan - Publishers

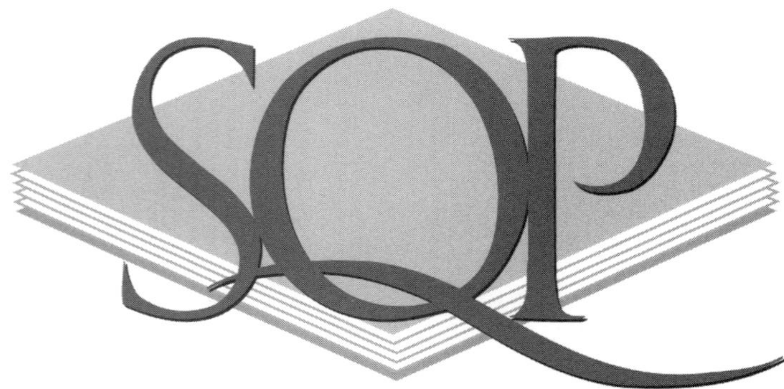

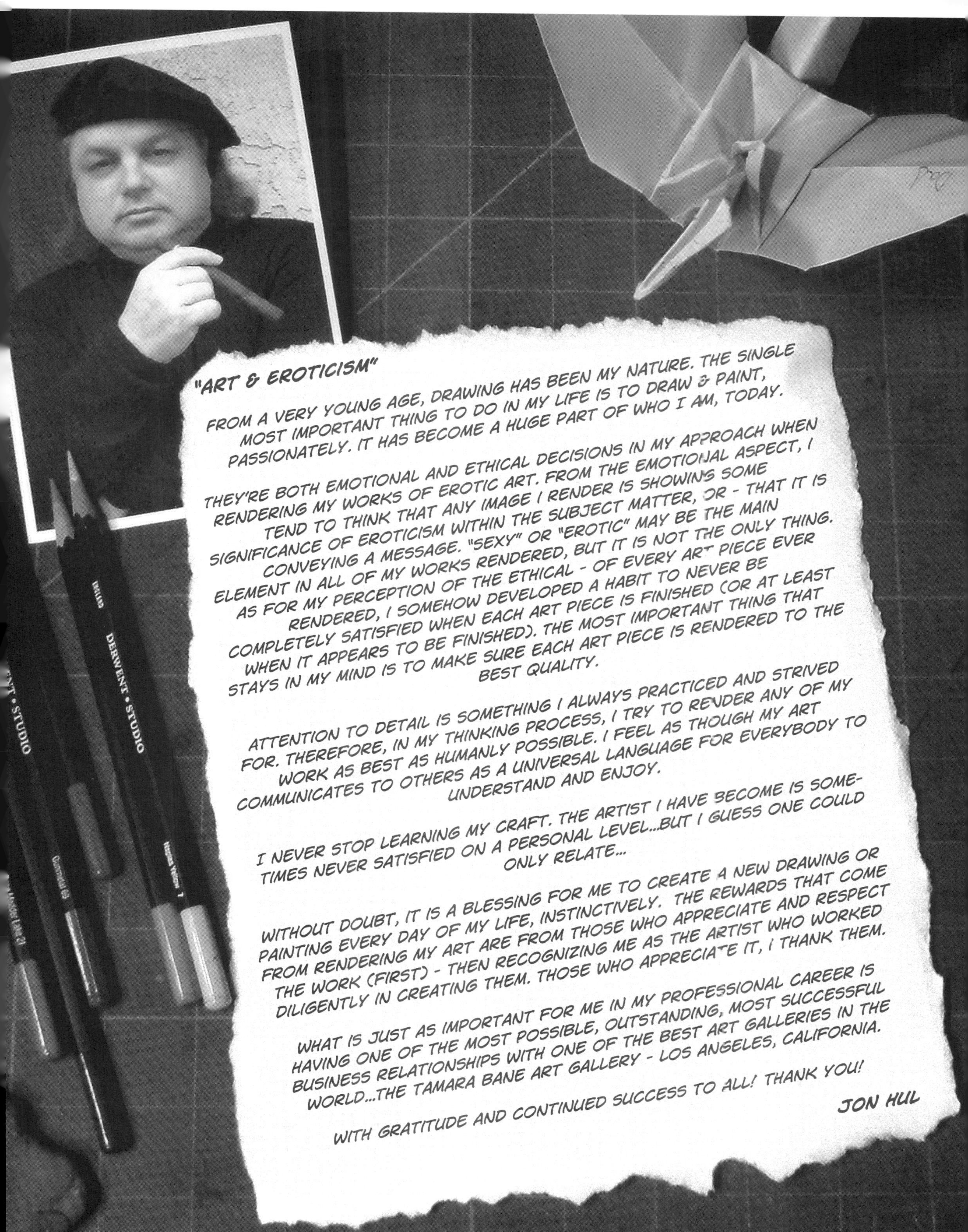

"ART & EROTICISM"

FROM A VERY YOUNG AGE, DRAWING HAS BEEN MY NATURE. THE SINGLE MOST IMPORTANT THING TO DO IN MY LIFE IS TO DRAW & PAINT, PASSIONATELY. IT HAS BECOME A HUGE PART OF WHO I AM, TODAY.

THEY'RE BOTH EMOTIONAL AND ETHICAL DECISIONS IN MY APPROACH WHEN RENDERING MY WORKS OF EROTIC ART. FROM THE EMOTIONAL ASPECT, I TEND TO THINK THAT ANY IMAGE I RENDER IS SHOWING SOME SIGNIFICANCE OF EROTICISM WITHIN THE SUBJECT MATTER, OR - THAT IT IS CONVEYING A MESSAGE. "SEXY" OR "EROTIC" MAY BE THE MAIN ELEMENT IN ALL OF MY WORKS RENDERED, BUT IT IS NOT THE ONLY THING. AS FOR MY PERCEPTION OF THE ETHICAL - OF EVERY ART PIECE EVER RENDERED, I SOMEHOW DEVELOPED A HABIT TO NEVER BE COMPLETELY SATISFIED WHEN EACH ART PIECE IS FINISHED (OR AT LEAST WHEN IT APPEARS TO BE FINISHED). THE MOST IMPORTANT THING THAT STAYS IN MY MIND IS TO MAKE SURE EACH ART PIECE IS RENDERED TO THE BEST QUALITY.

ATTENTION TO DETAIL IS SOMETHING I ALWAYS PRACTICED AND STRIVED FOR. THEREFORE, IN MY THINKING PROCESS, I TRY TO RENDER ANY OF MY WORK AS BEST AS HUMANLY POSSIBLE. I FEEL AS THOUGH MY ART COMMUNICATES TO OTHERS AS A UNIVERSAL LANGUAGE FOR EVERYBODY TO UNDERSTAND AND ENJOY.

I NEVER STOP LEARNING MY CRAFT. THE ARTIST I HAVE BECOME IS SOME-TIMES NEVER SATISFIED ON A PERSONAL LEVEL...BUT I GUESS ONE COULD ONLY RELATE...

WITHOUT DOUBT, IT IS A BLESSING FOR ME TO CREATE A NEW DRAWING OR PAINTING EVERY DAY OF MY LIFE, INSTINCTIVELY. THE REWARDS THAT COME FROM RENDERING MY ART ARE FROM THOSE WHO APPRECIATE AND RESPECT THE WORK (FIRST) - THEN RECOGNIZING ME AS THE ARTIST WHO WORKED DILIGENTLY IN CREATING THEM. THOSE WHO APPRECIATE IT, I THANK THEM.

WHAT IS JUST AS IMPORTANT FOR ME IN MY PROFESSIONAL CAREER IS HAVING ONE OF THE MOST POSSIBLE, OUTSTANDING, MOST SUCCESSFUL BUSINESS RELATIONSHIPS WITH ONE OF THE BEST ART GALLERIES IN THE WORLD...THE TAMARA BANE ART GALLERY - LOS ANGELES, CALIFORNIA.

WITH GRATITUDE AND CONTINUED SUCCESS TO ALL! THANK YOU!

JON HUL

For my Best Friend,
and to the Rest of my
Family... I love you!

OXOX

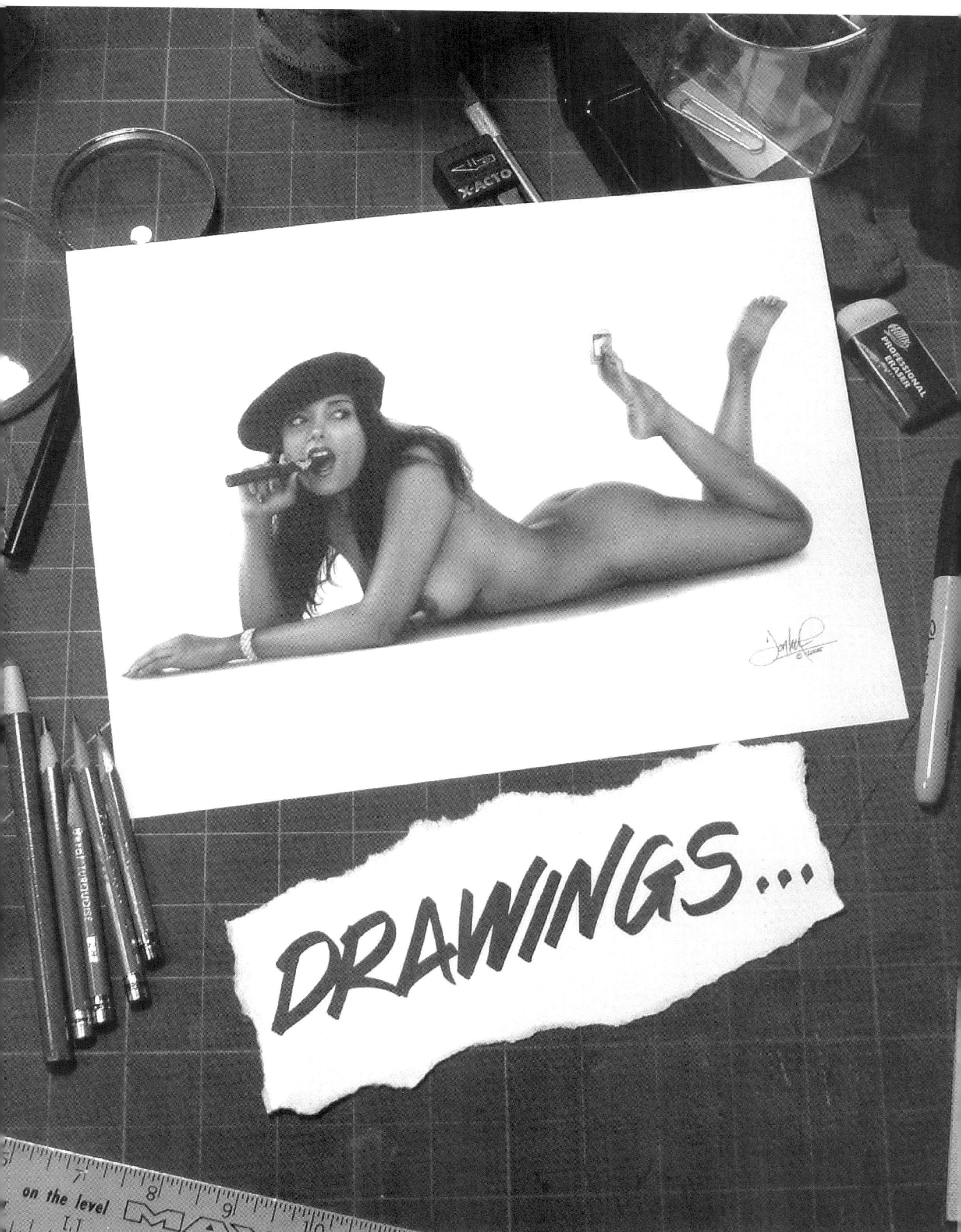
X-ACTO
PROFESSIONAL ERASER
DRAWINGS...
on the level

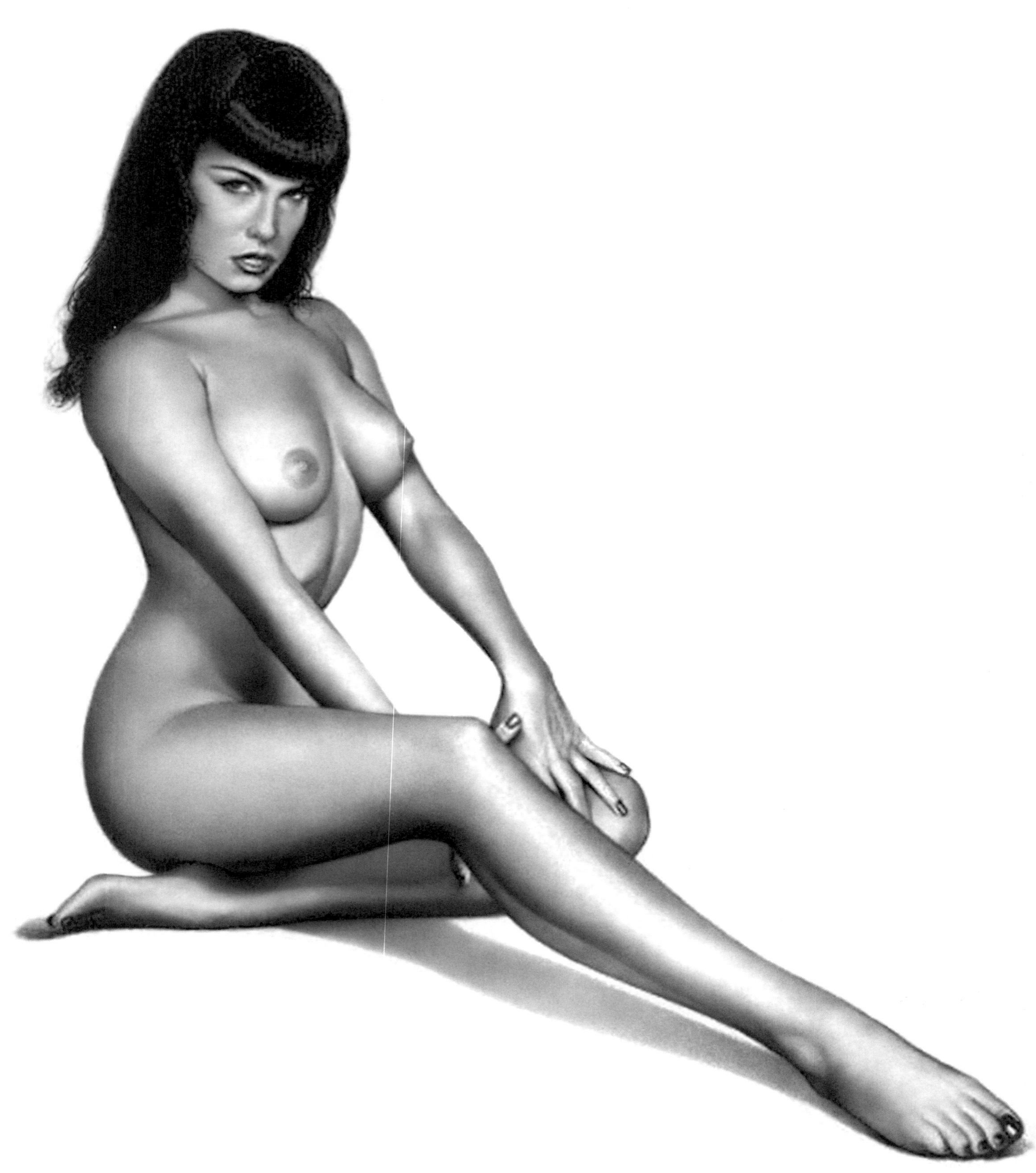

JON HUL
2000

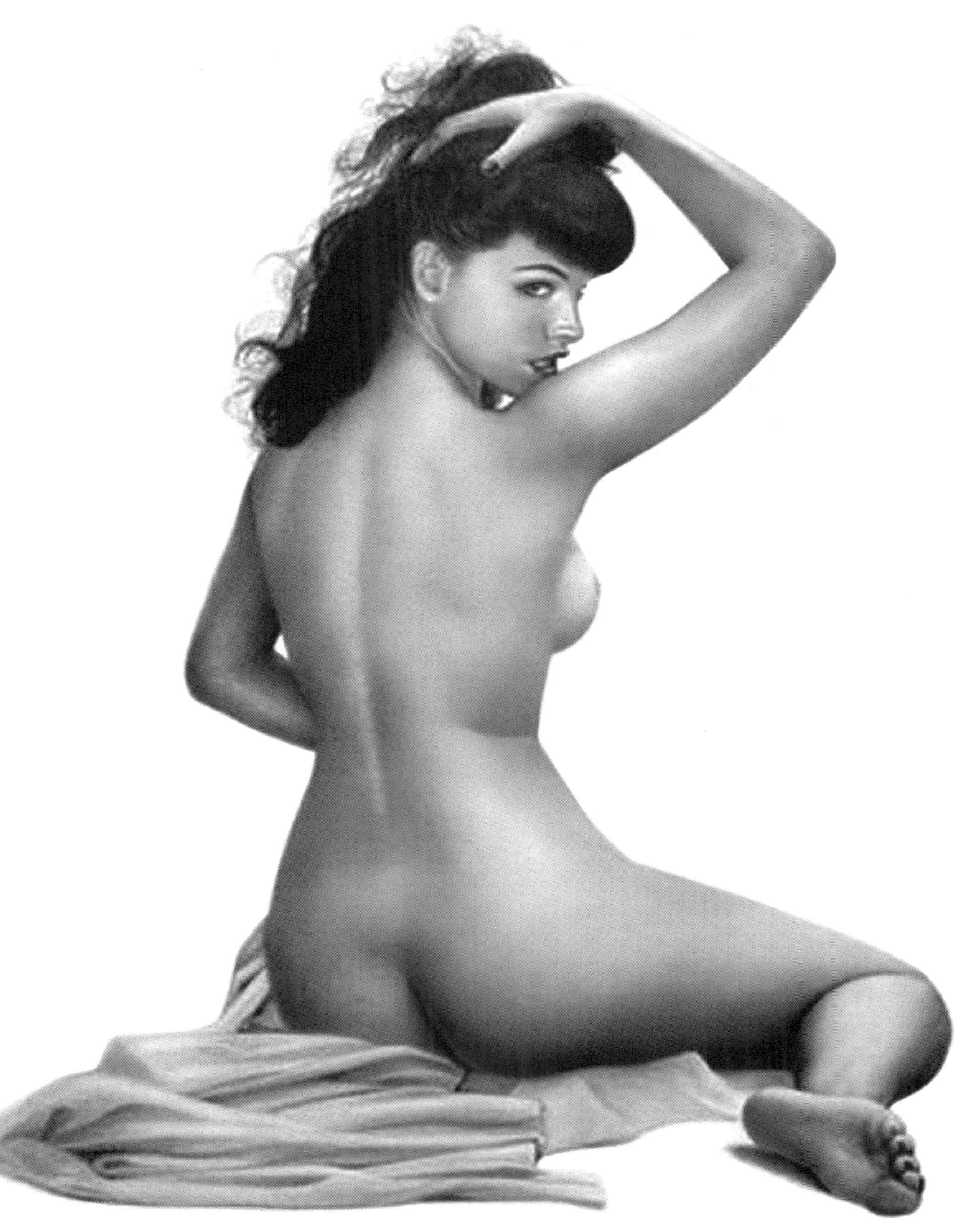

JON HUL
2000

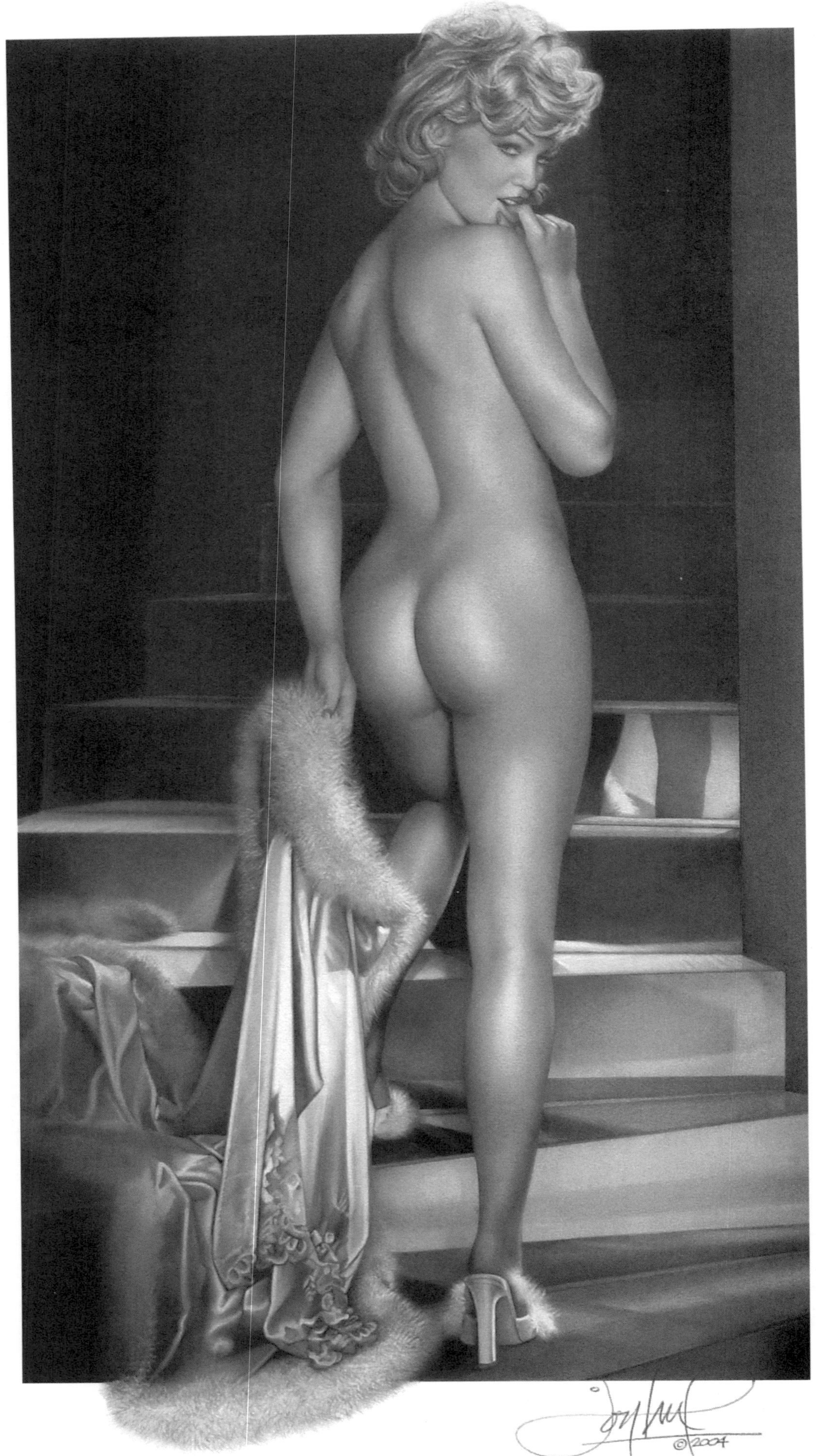

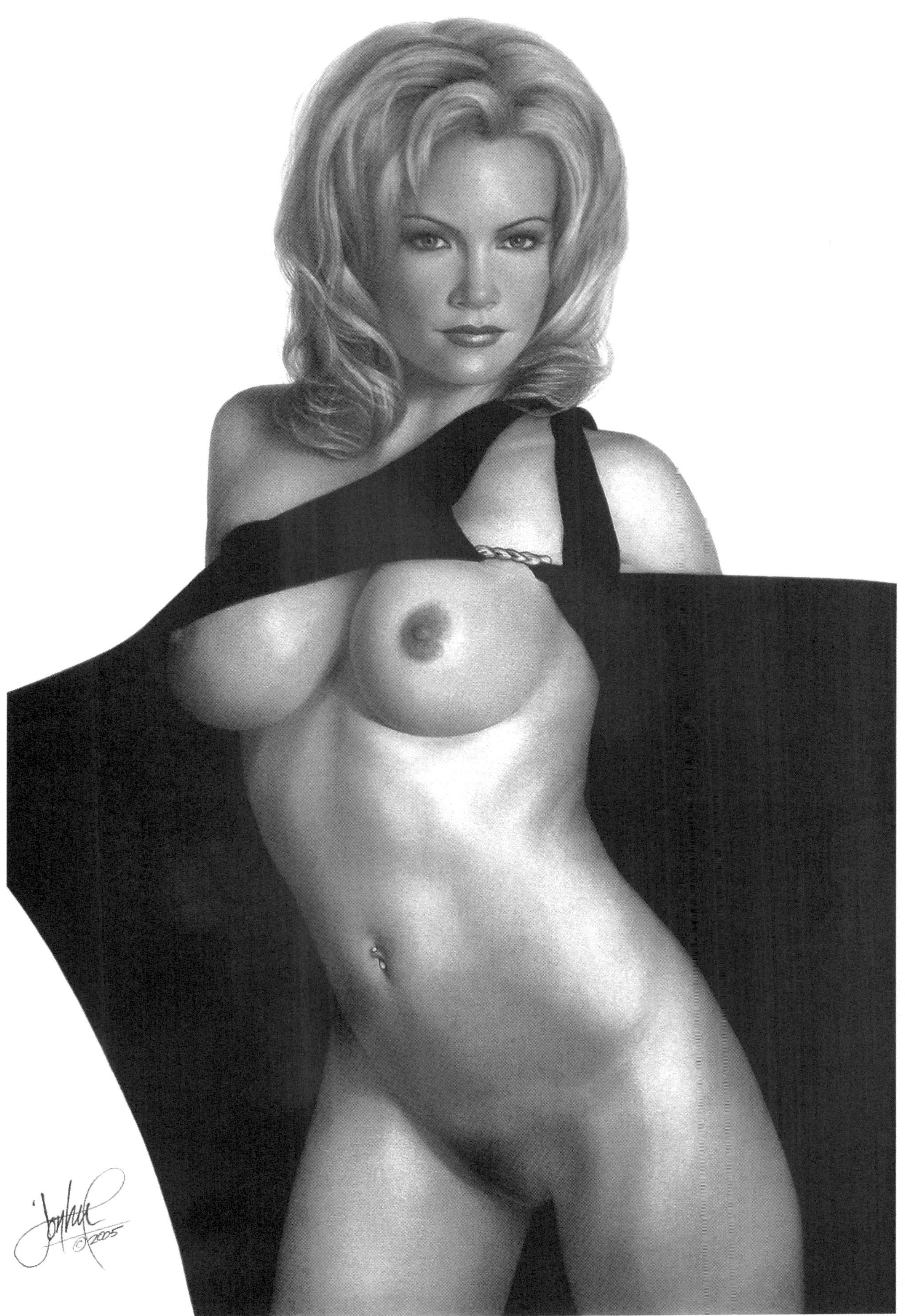

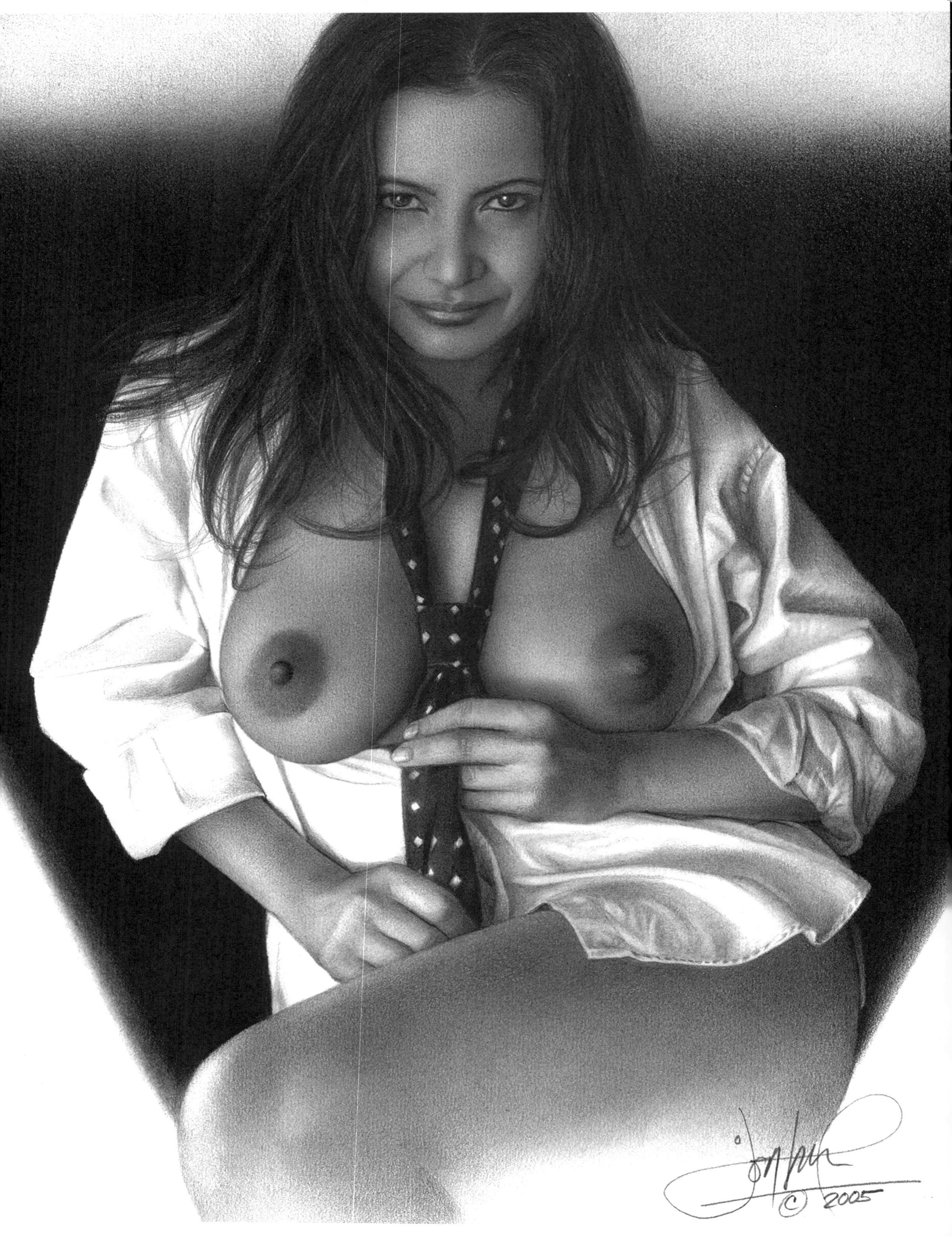
© 2005

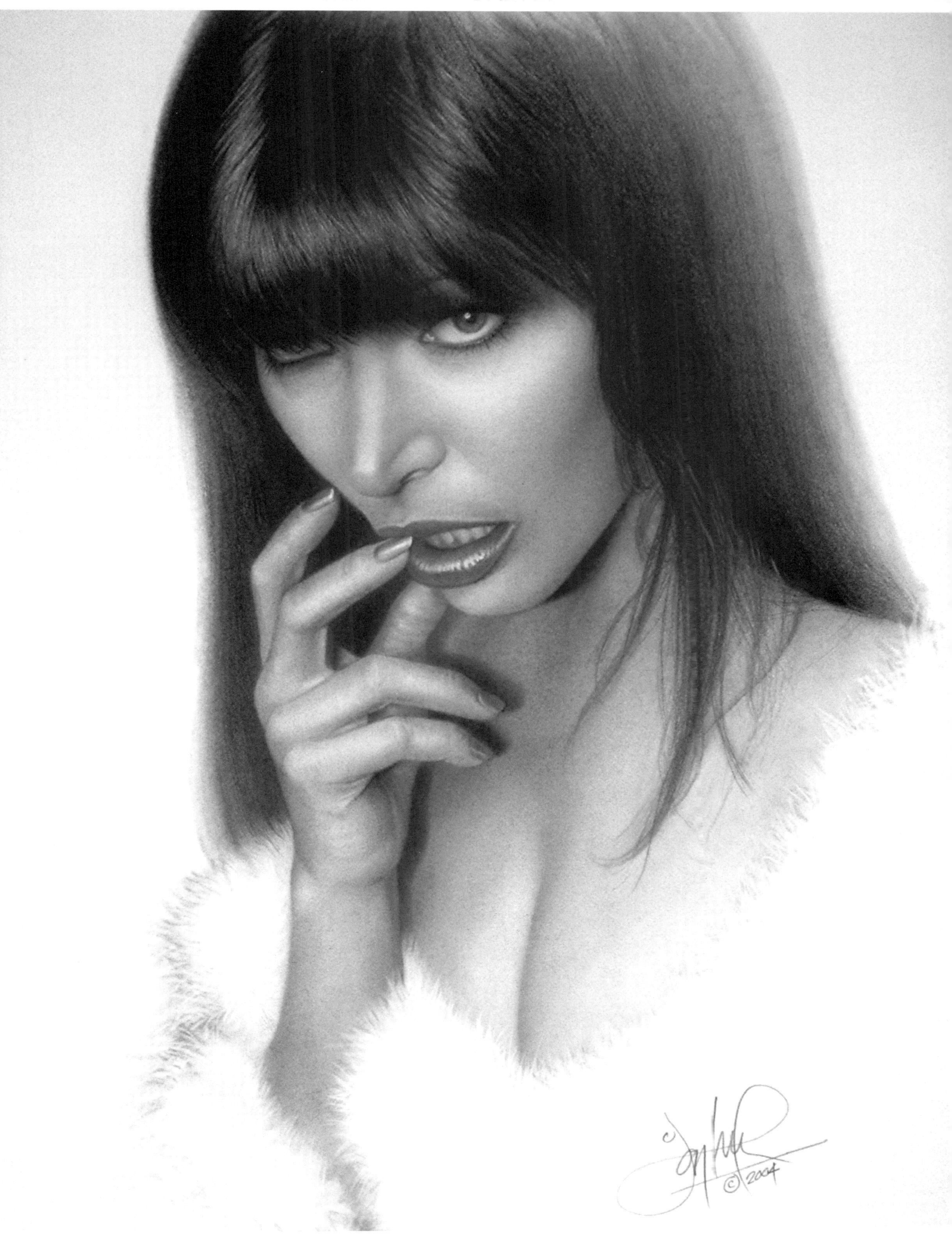
©2004

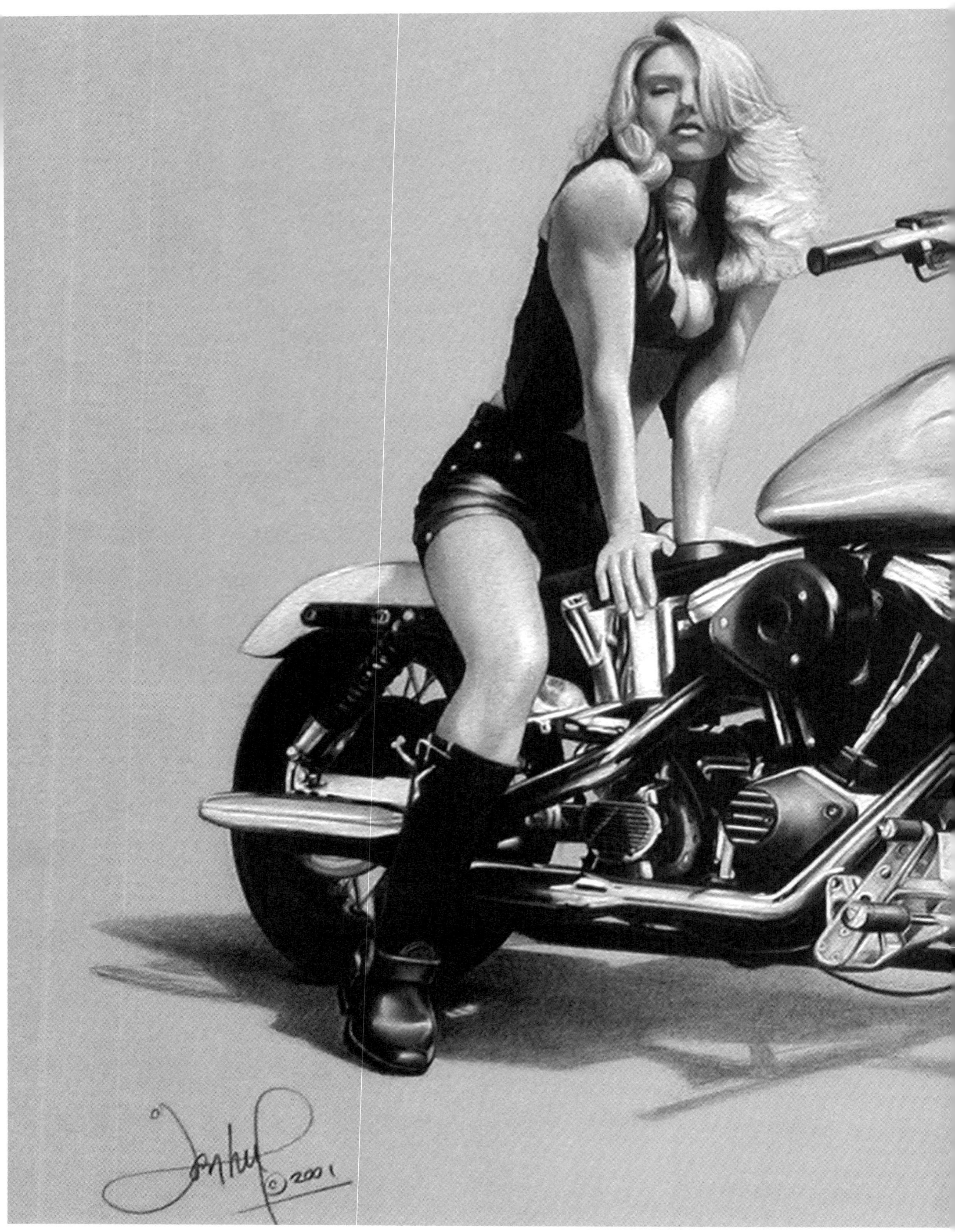
©2001

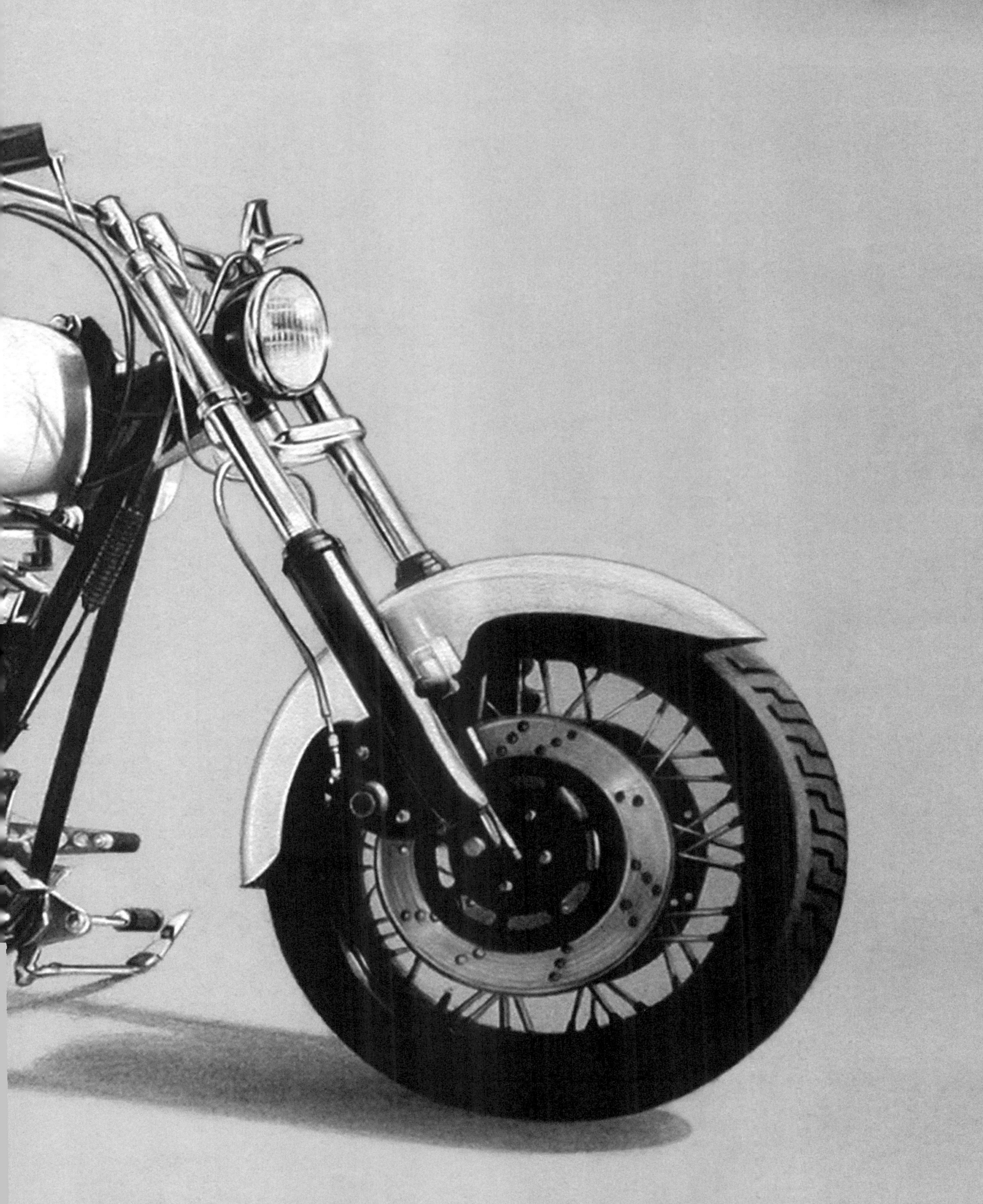

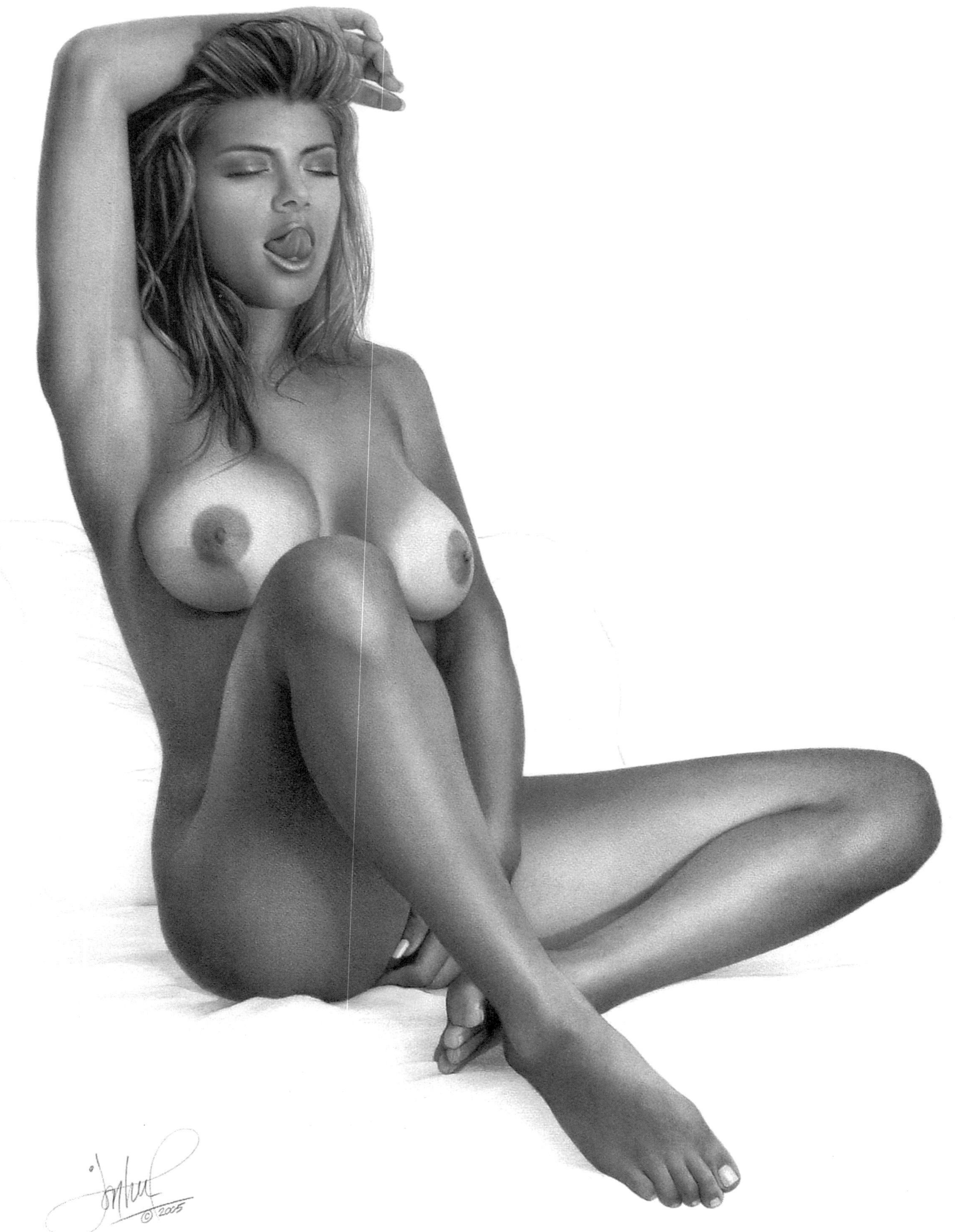
© 2005

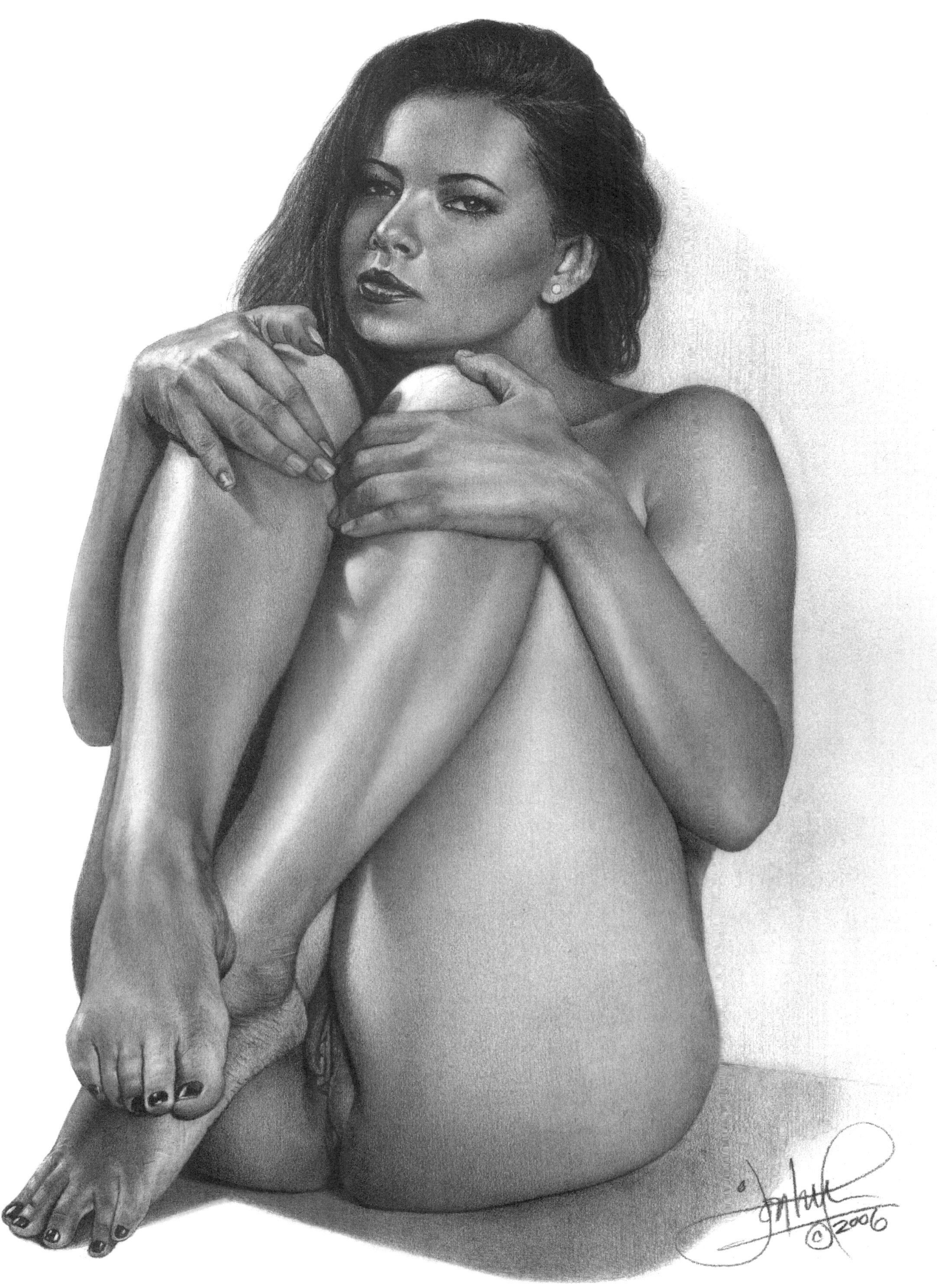
©2006

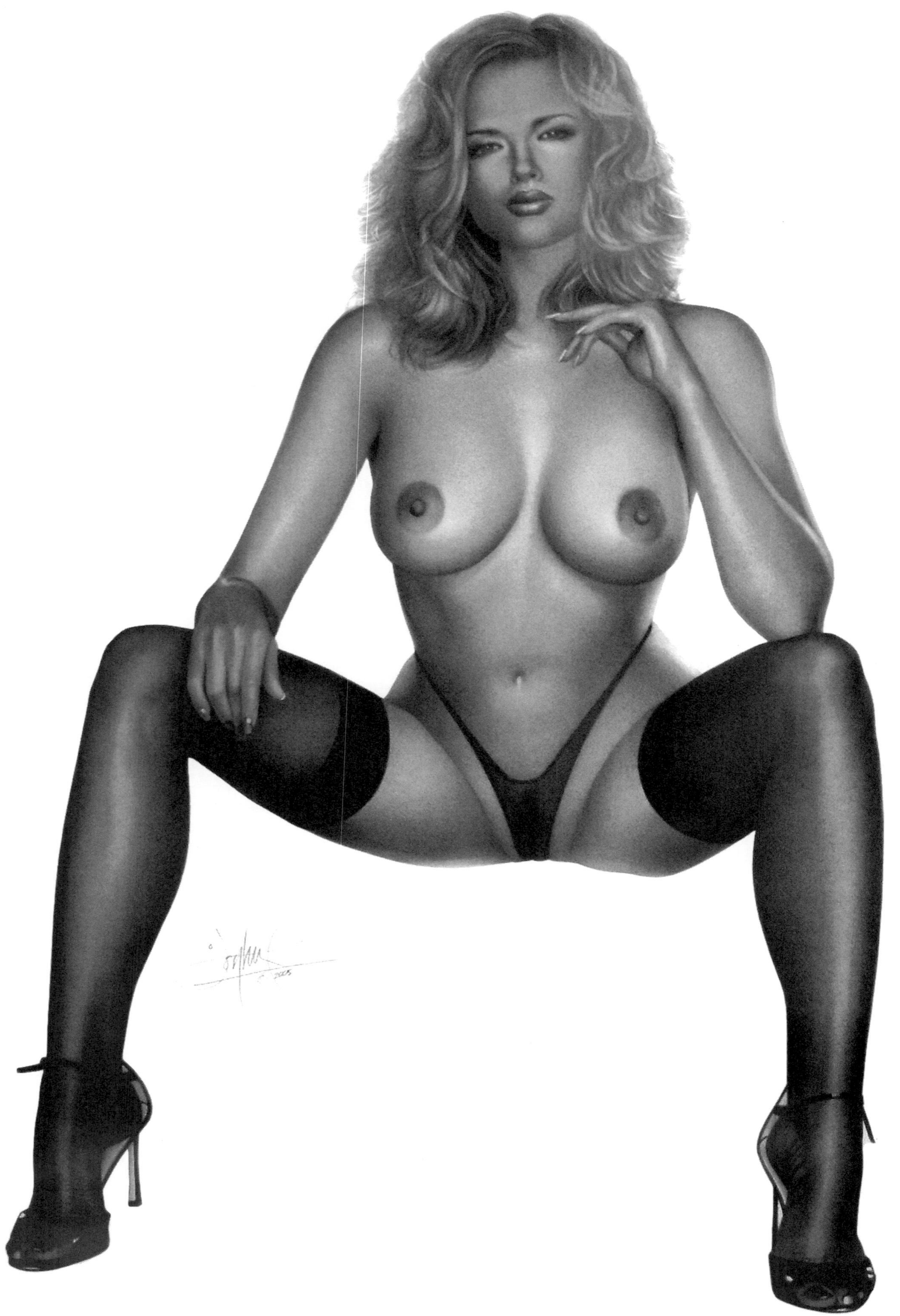

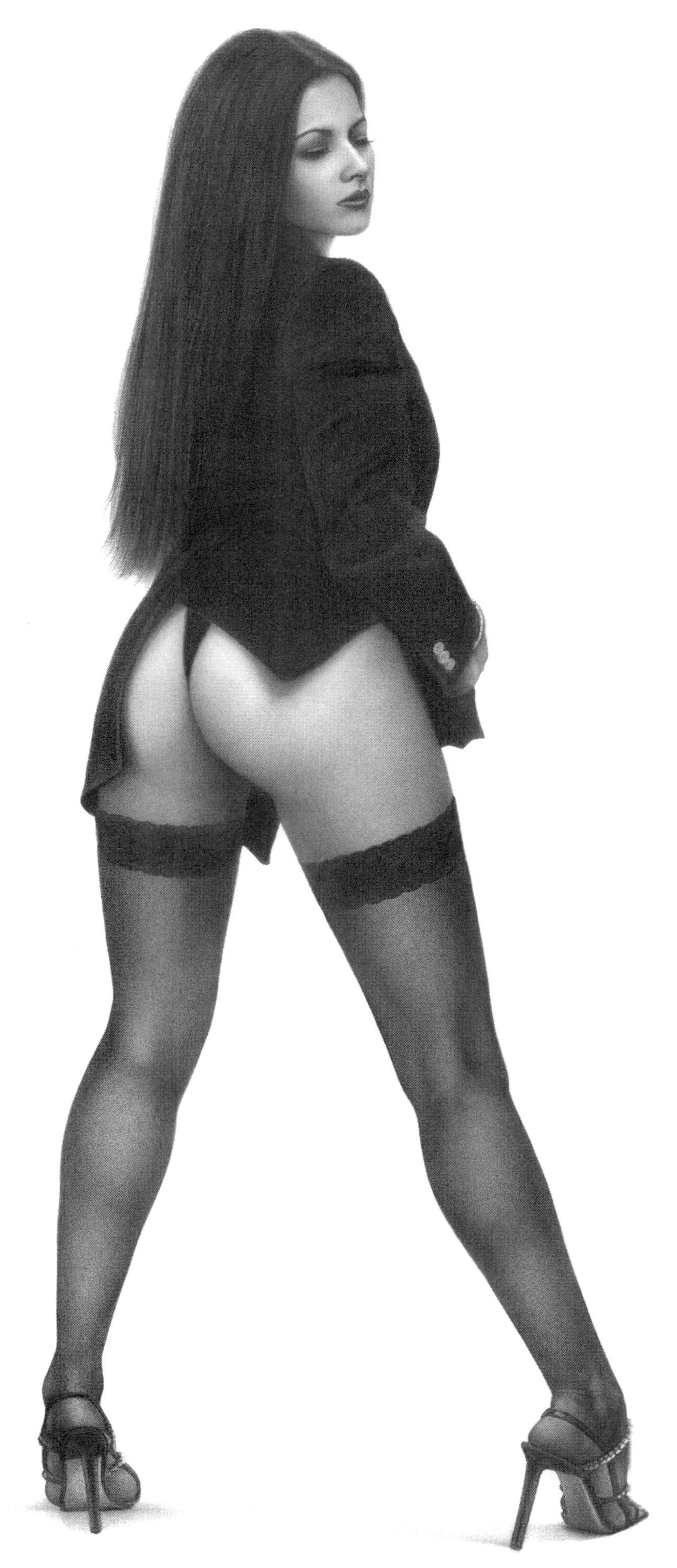

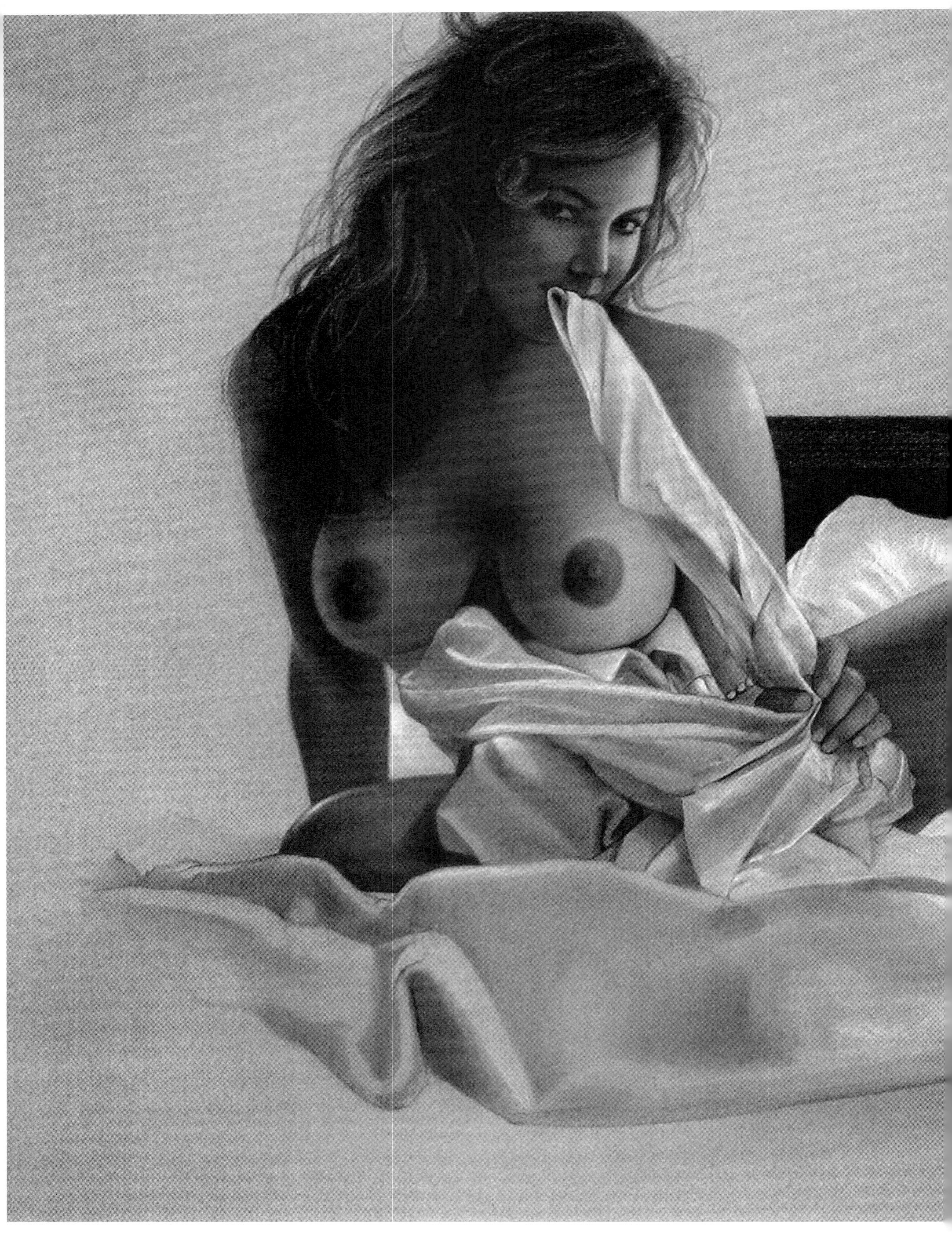

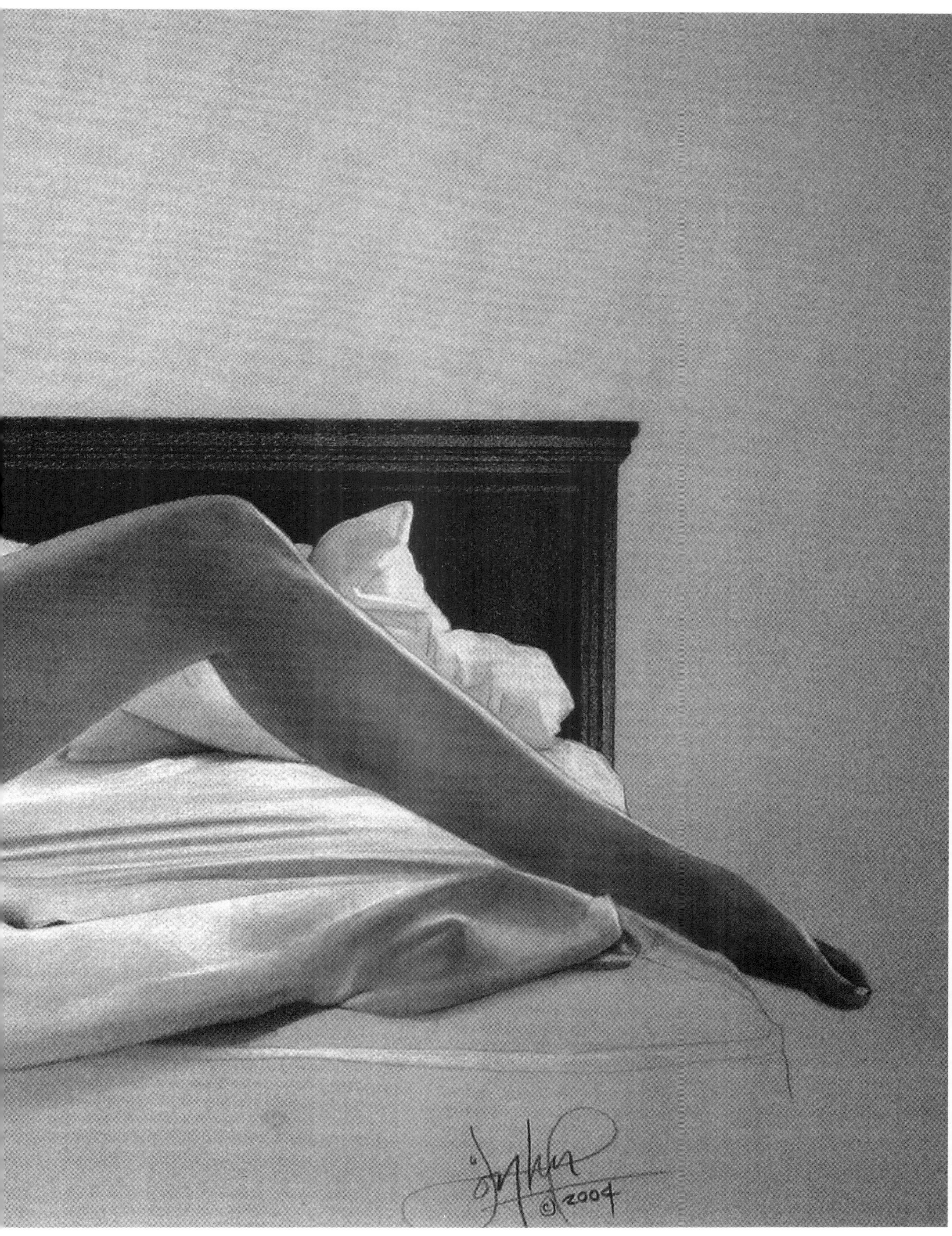
©2004

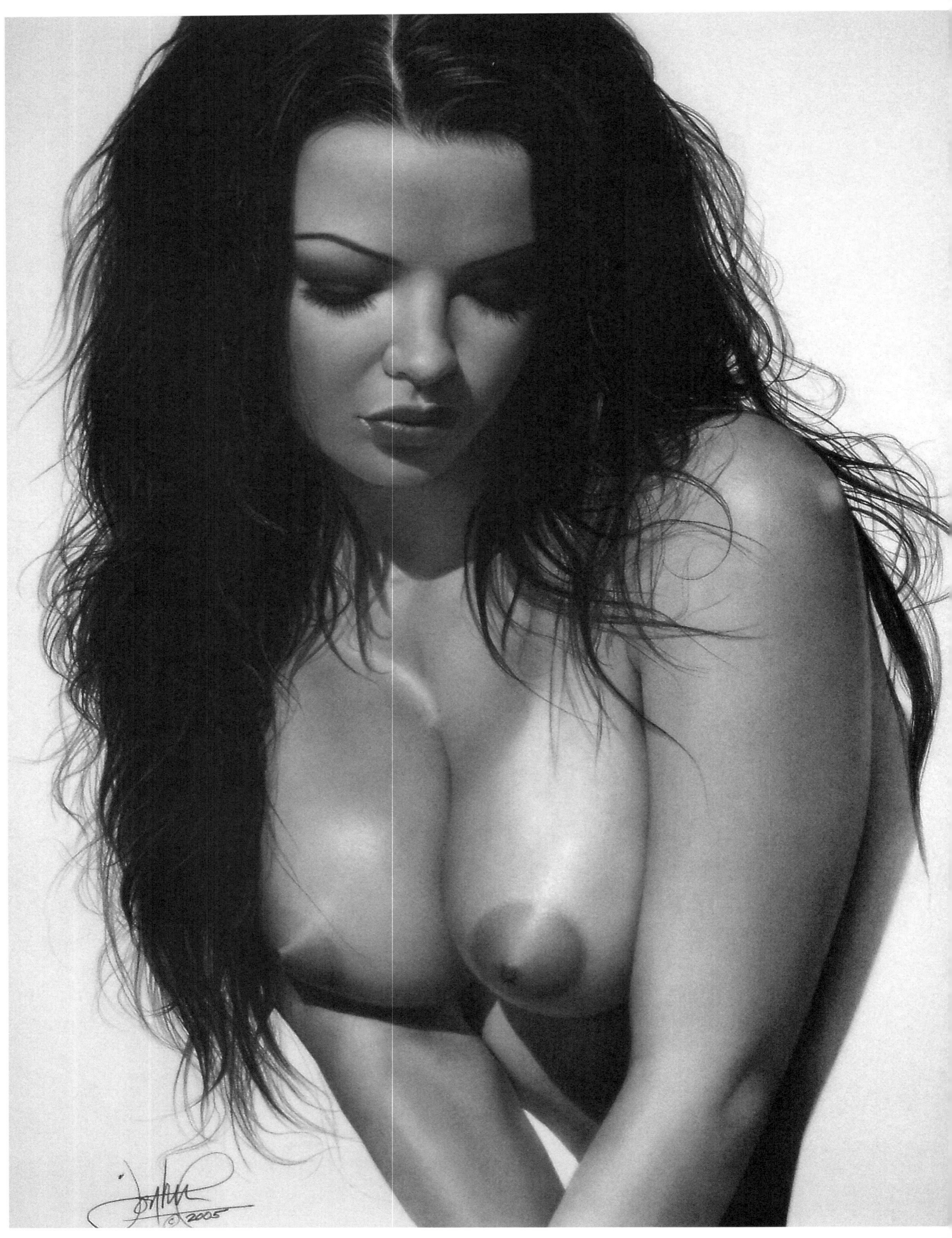
© 2005

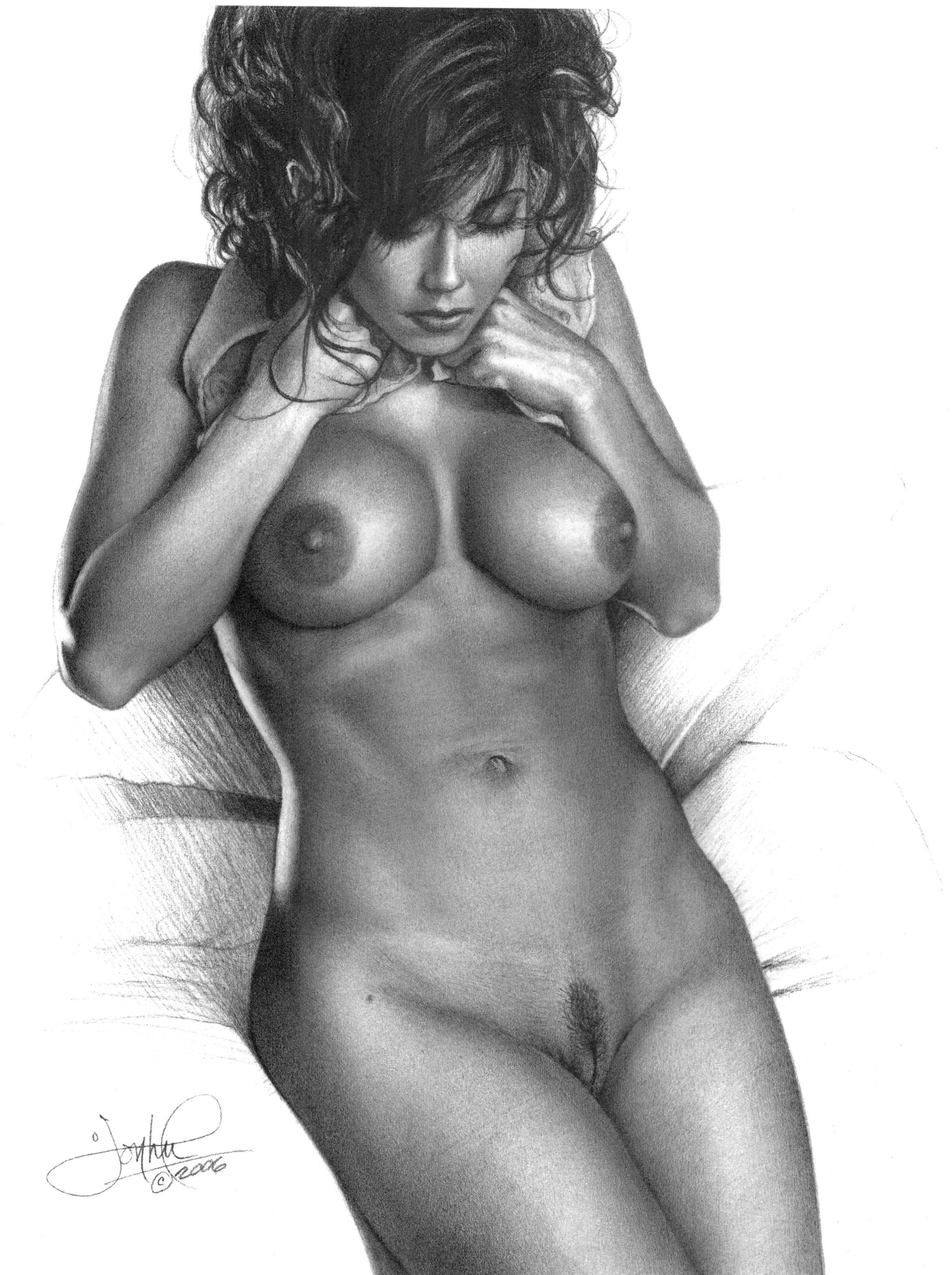
©2006

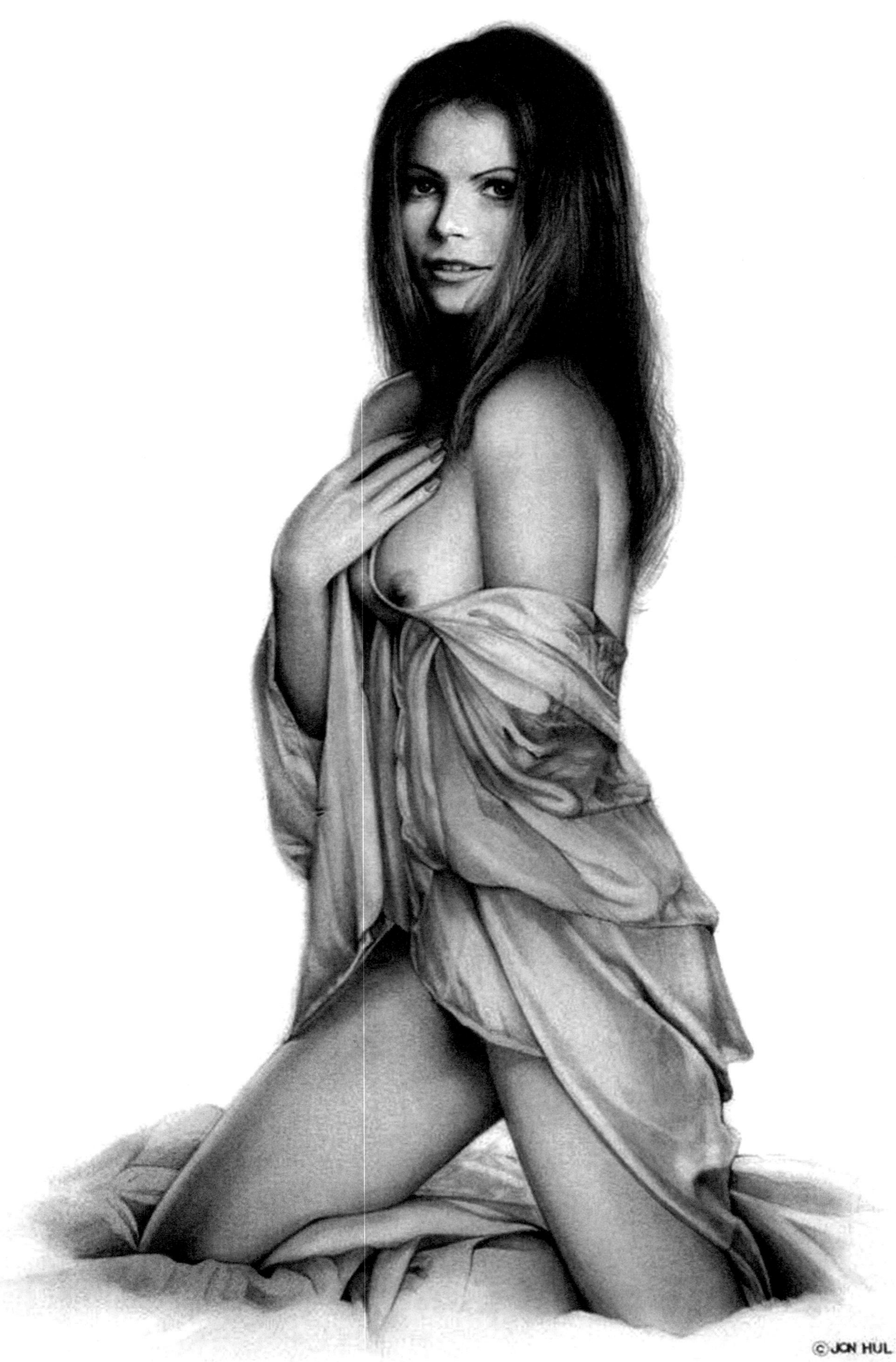
© JON HUL '98

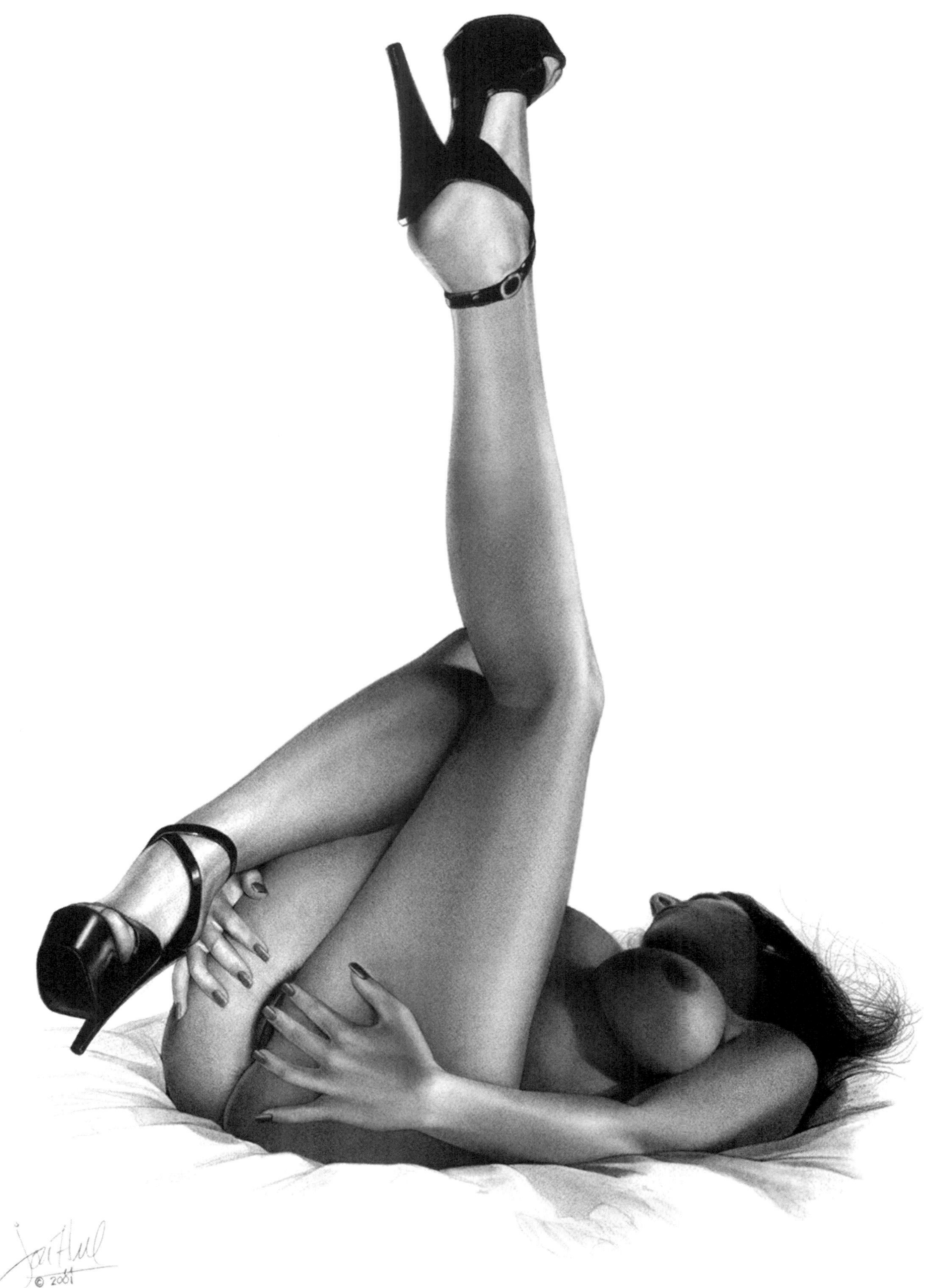
© 2001

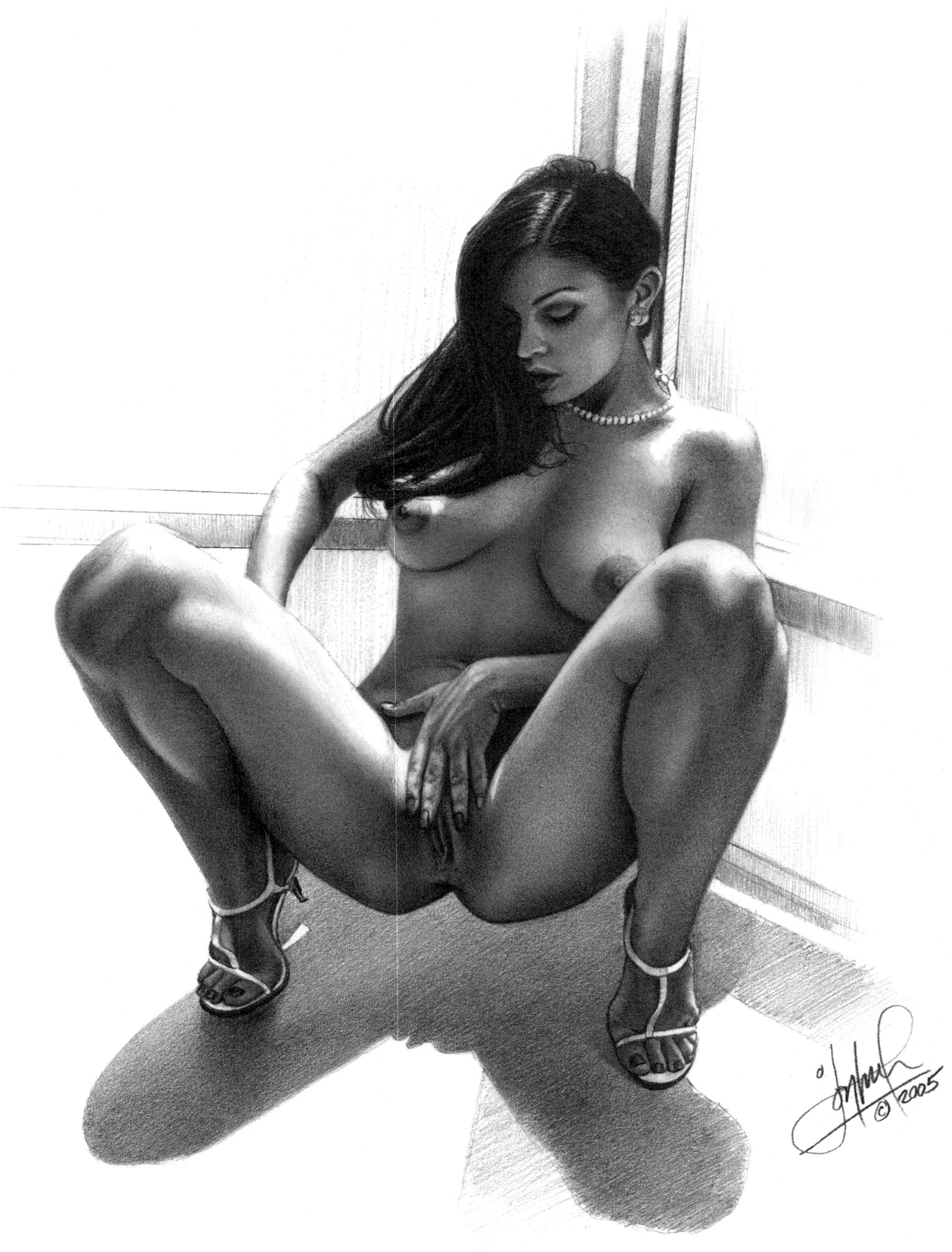
© 2005

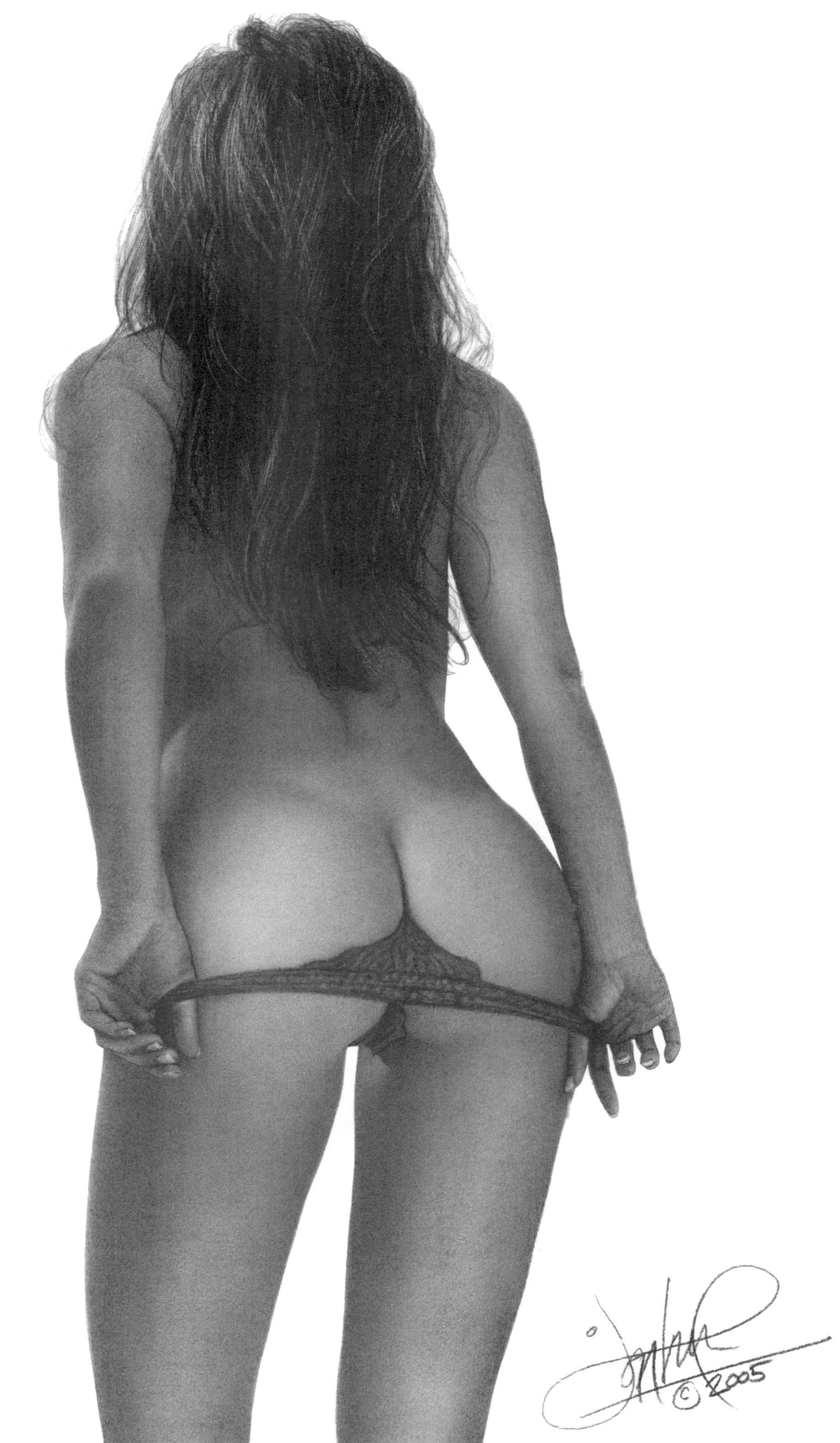
© 2005

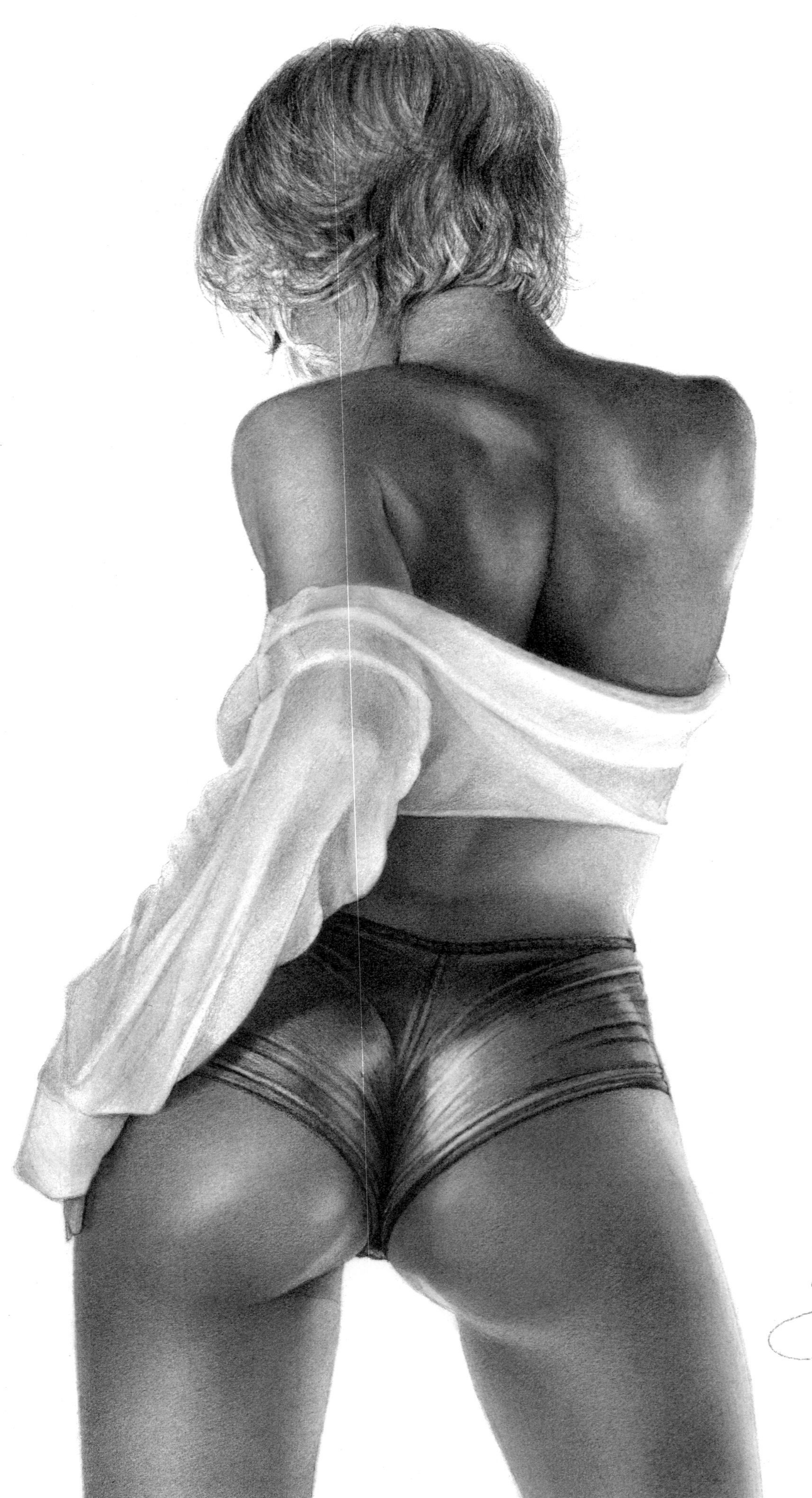
© 2005

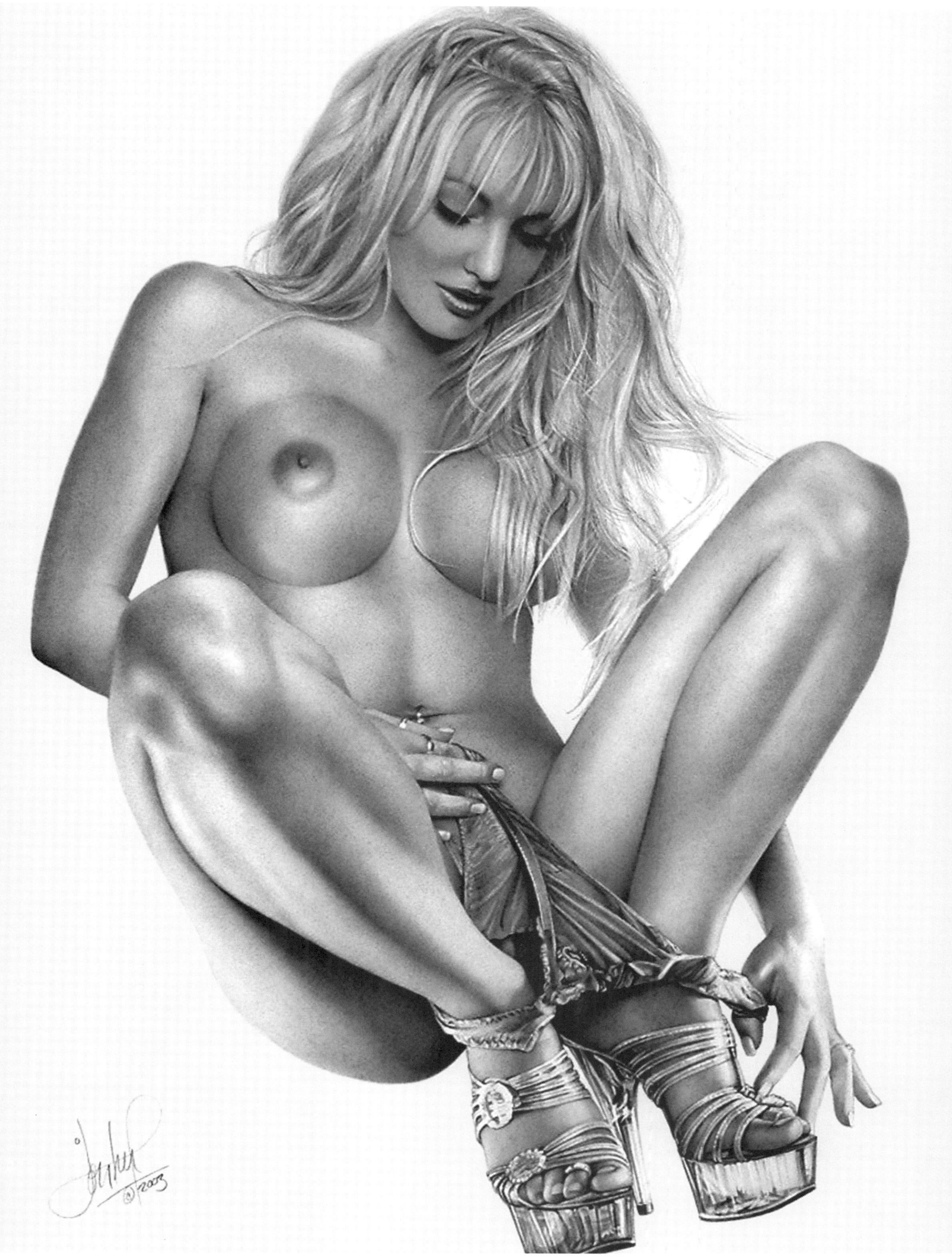

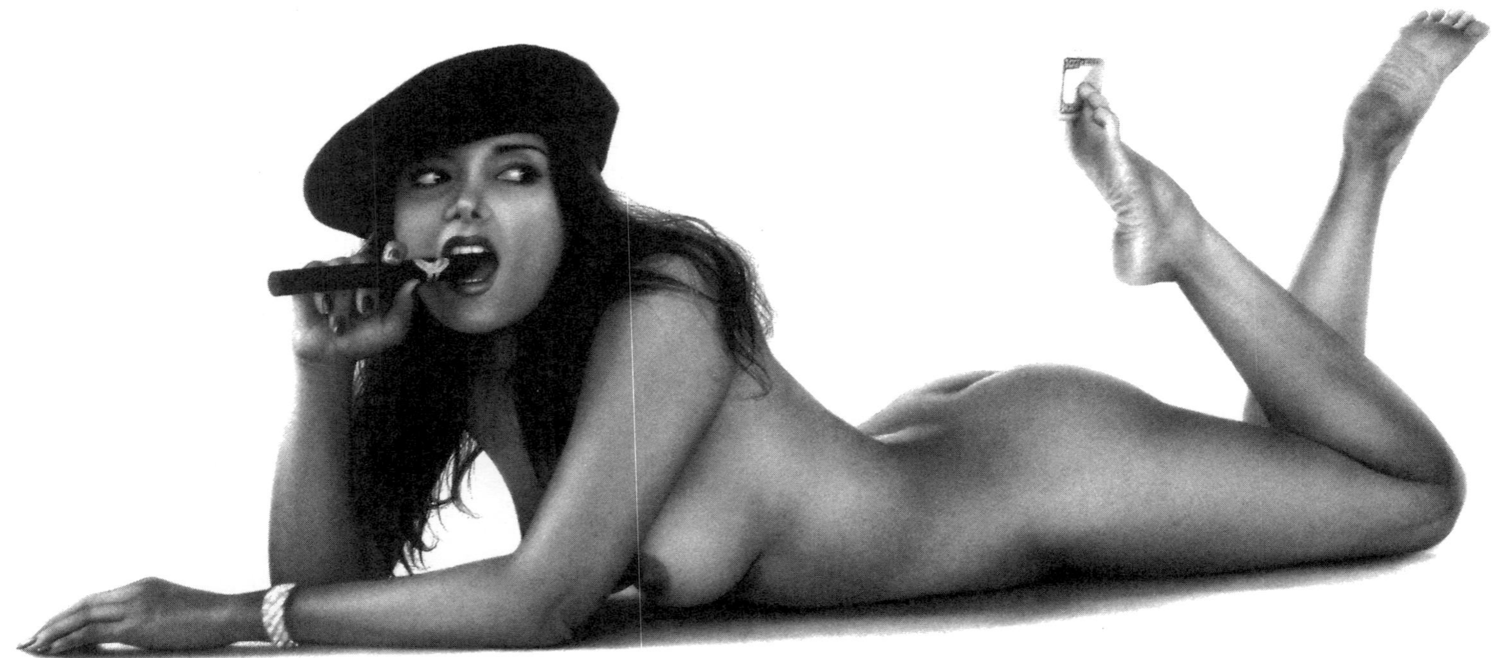

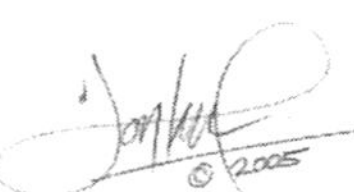

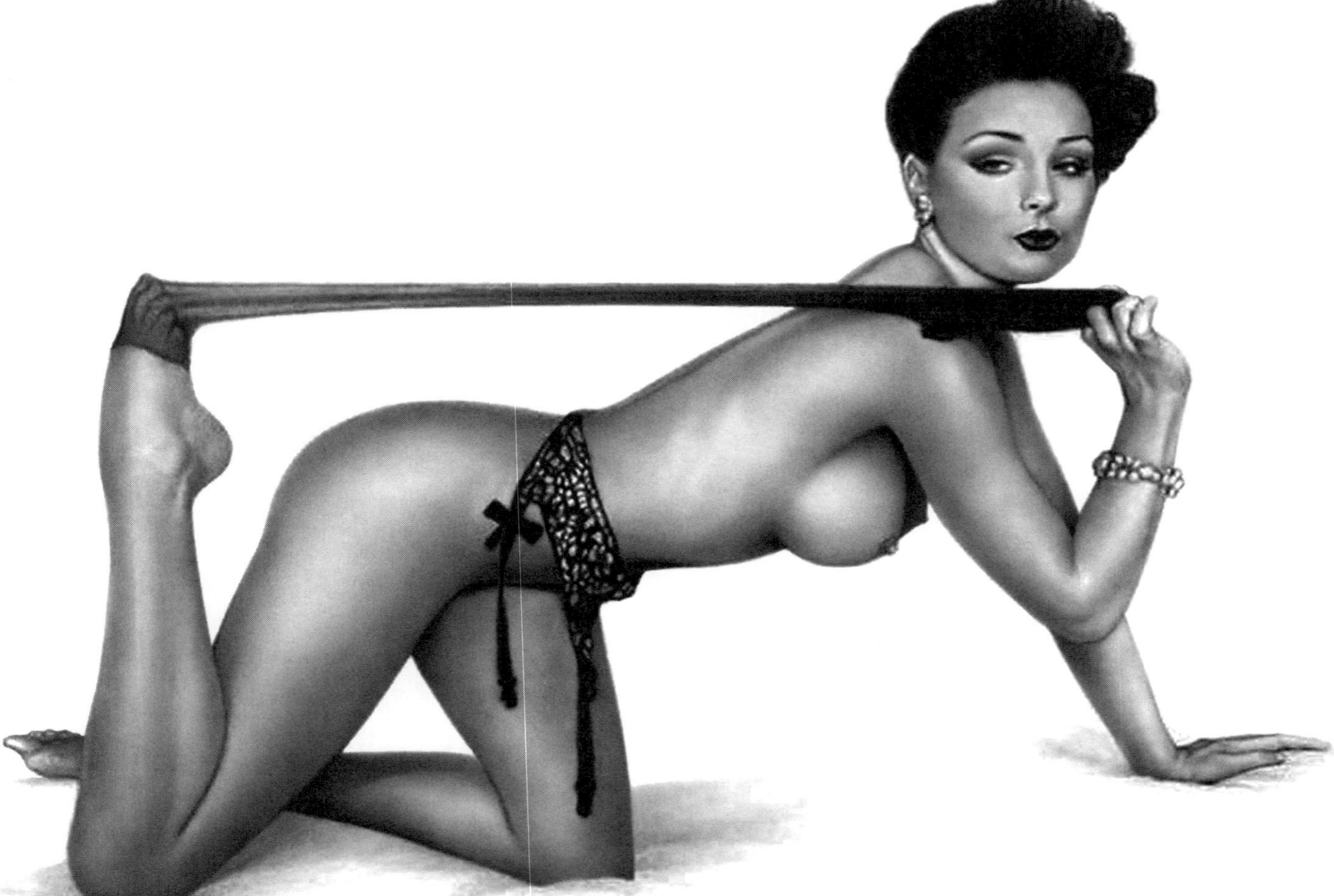

jon hul
2000

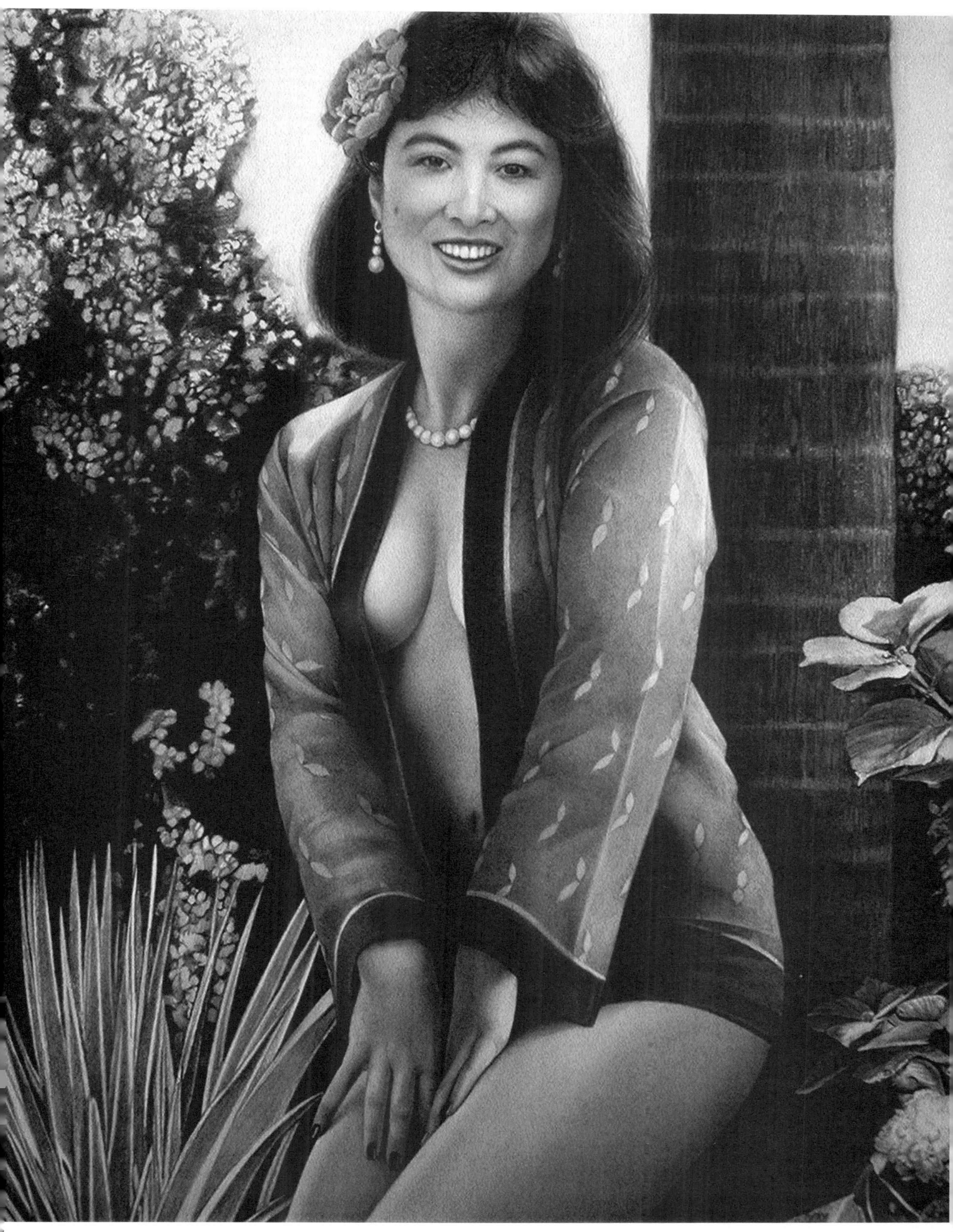

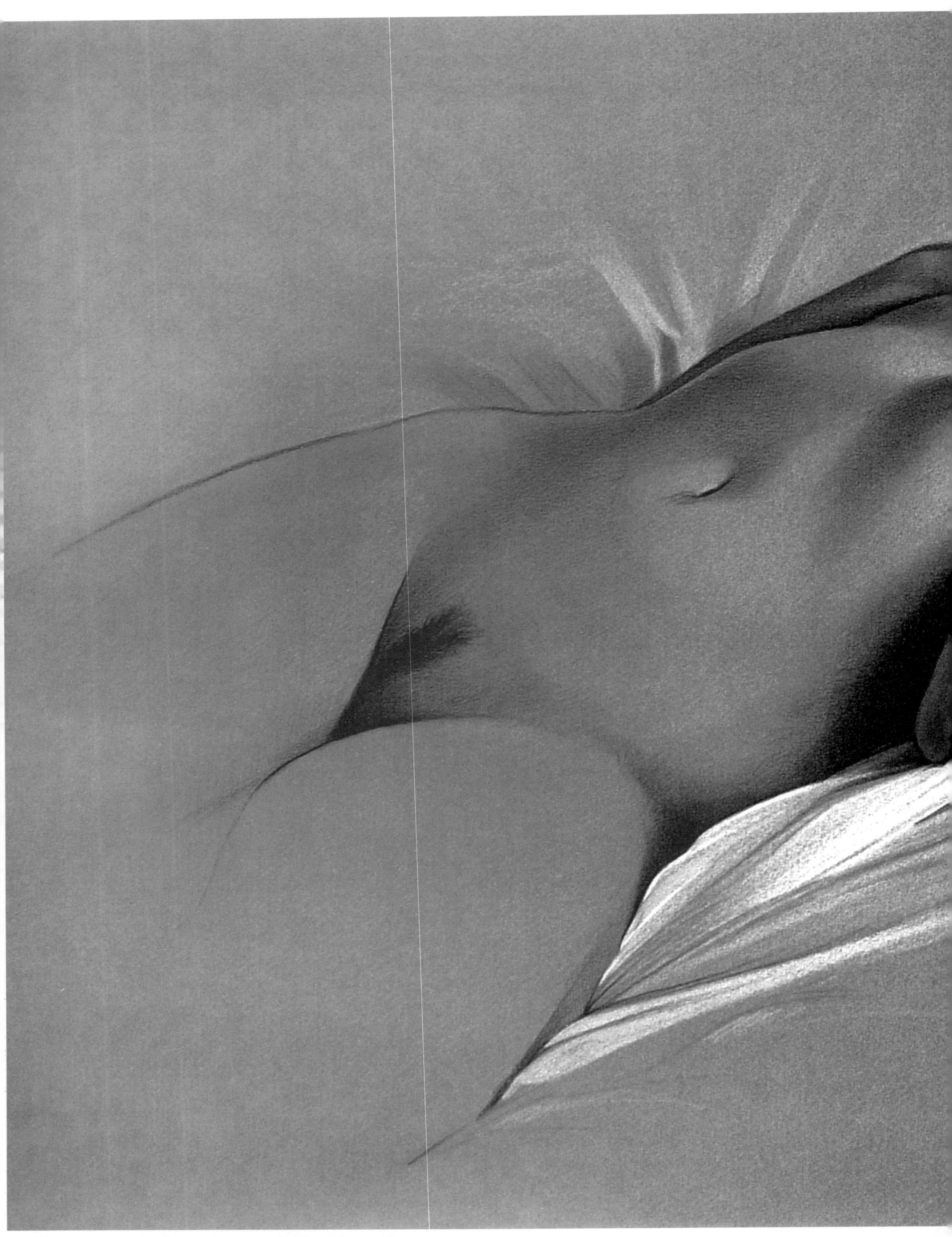

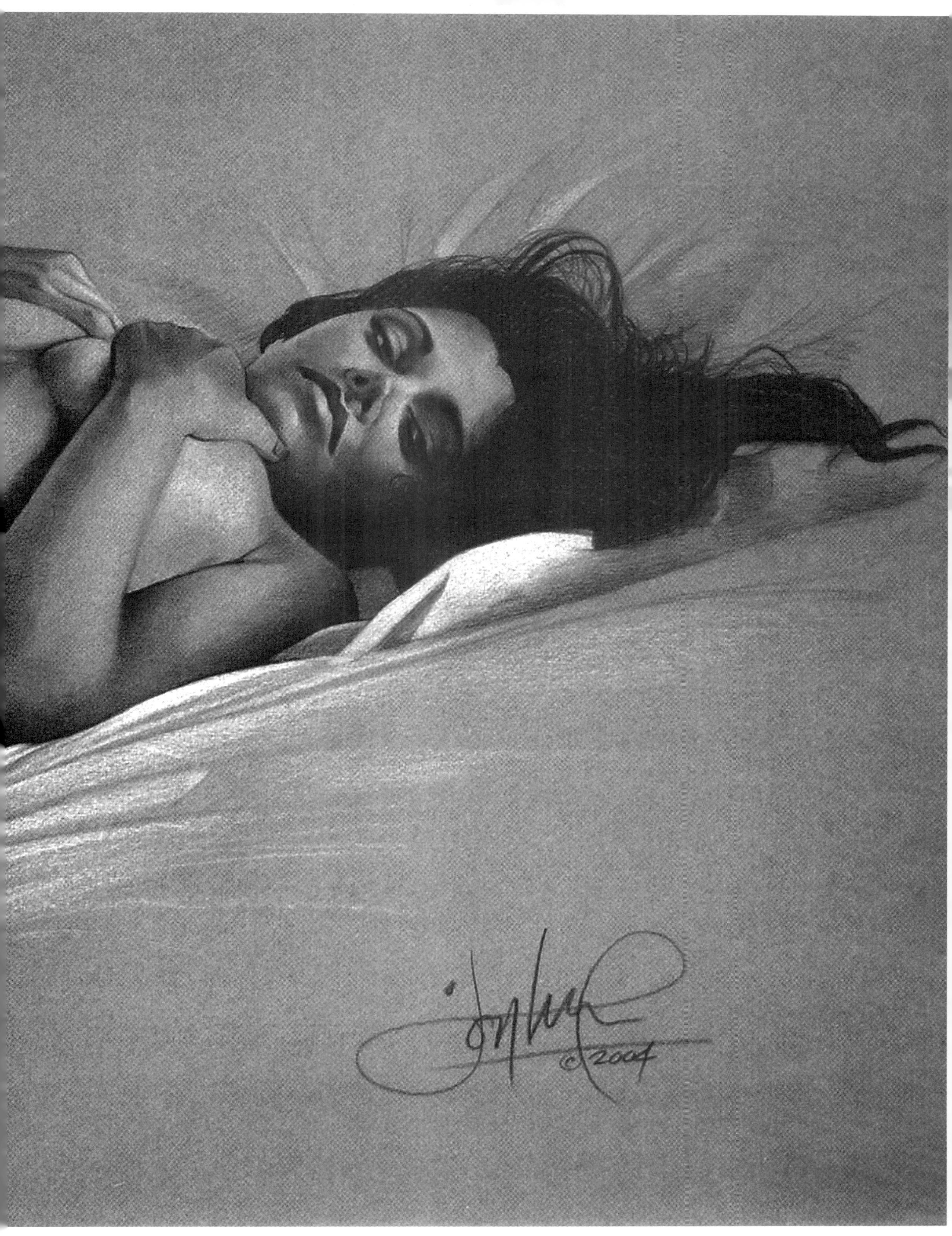
©2004

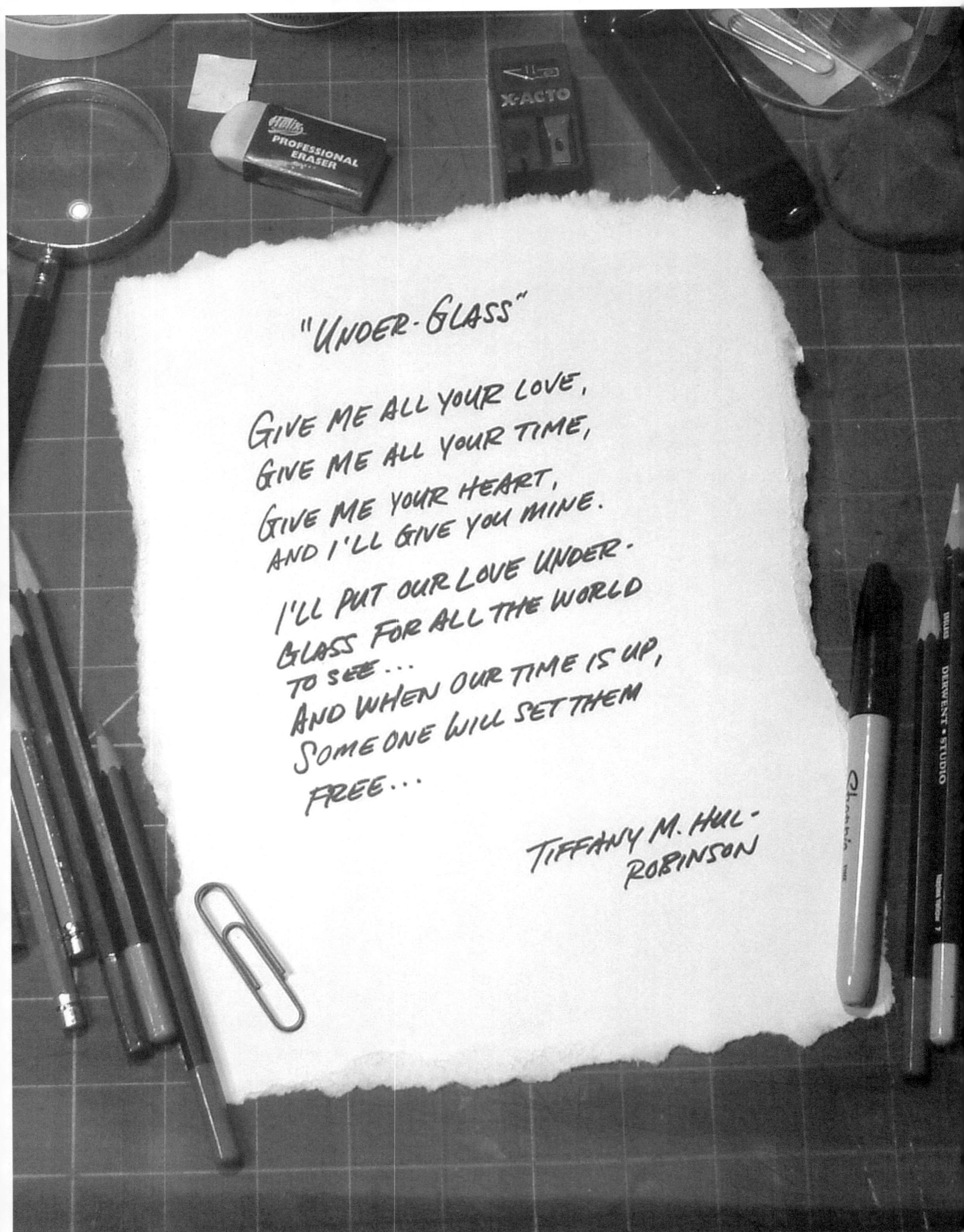
PROFESSIONAL ERASER
X-ACTO
"UNDER-GLASS"
GIVE ME ALL YOUR LOVE,
GIVE ME ALL YOUR TIME,
GIVE ME YOUR HEART,
AND I'LL GIVE YOU MINE.
I'LL PUT OUR LOVE UNDER-
GLASS FOR ALL THE WORLD
TO SEE...
AND WHEN OUR TIME IS UP,
SOME ONE WILL SET THEM
FREE...
TIFFANY M. HUL-
ROBINSON
DERWENT • STUDIO

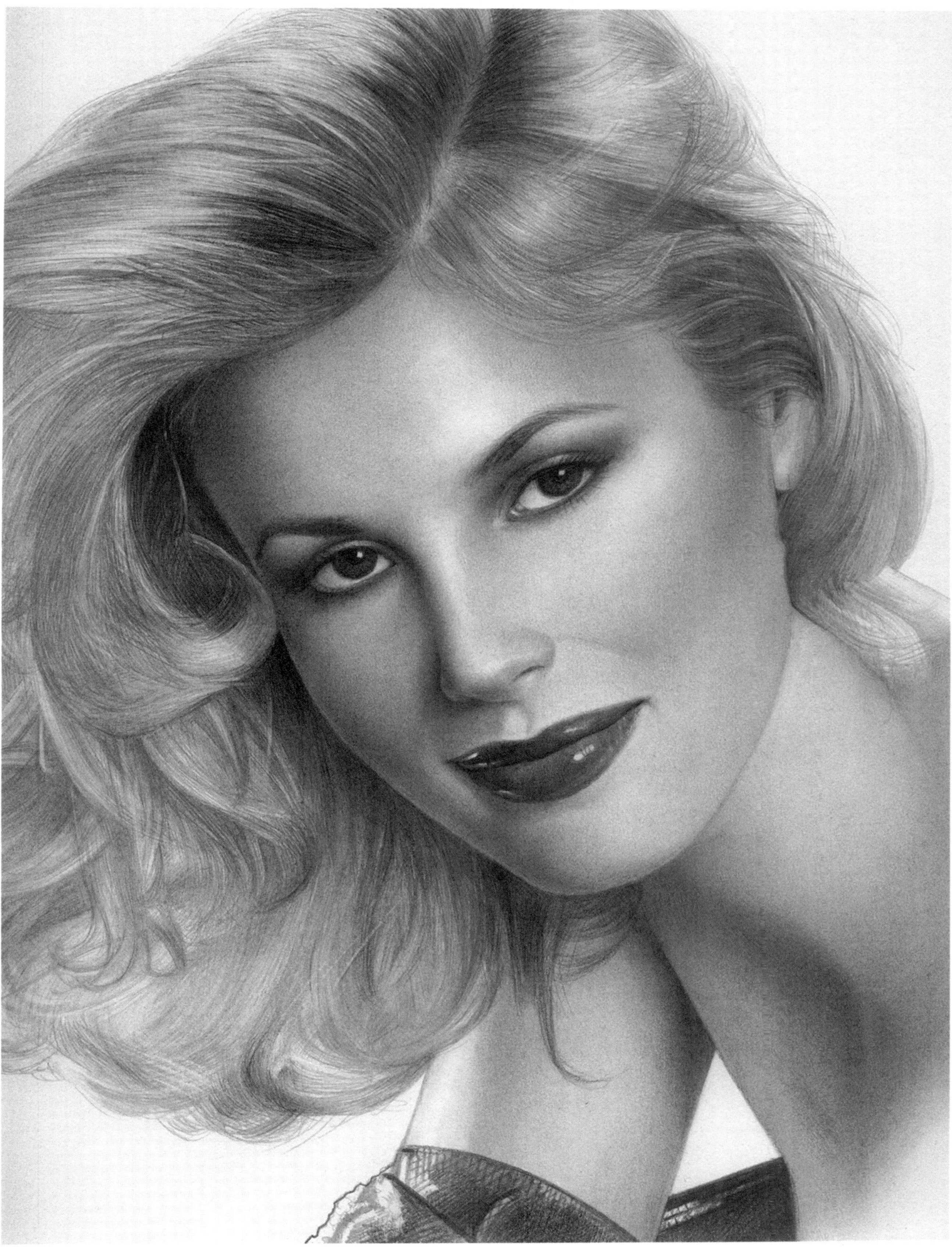

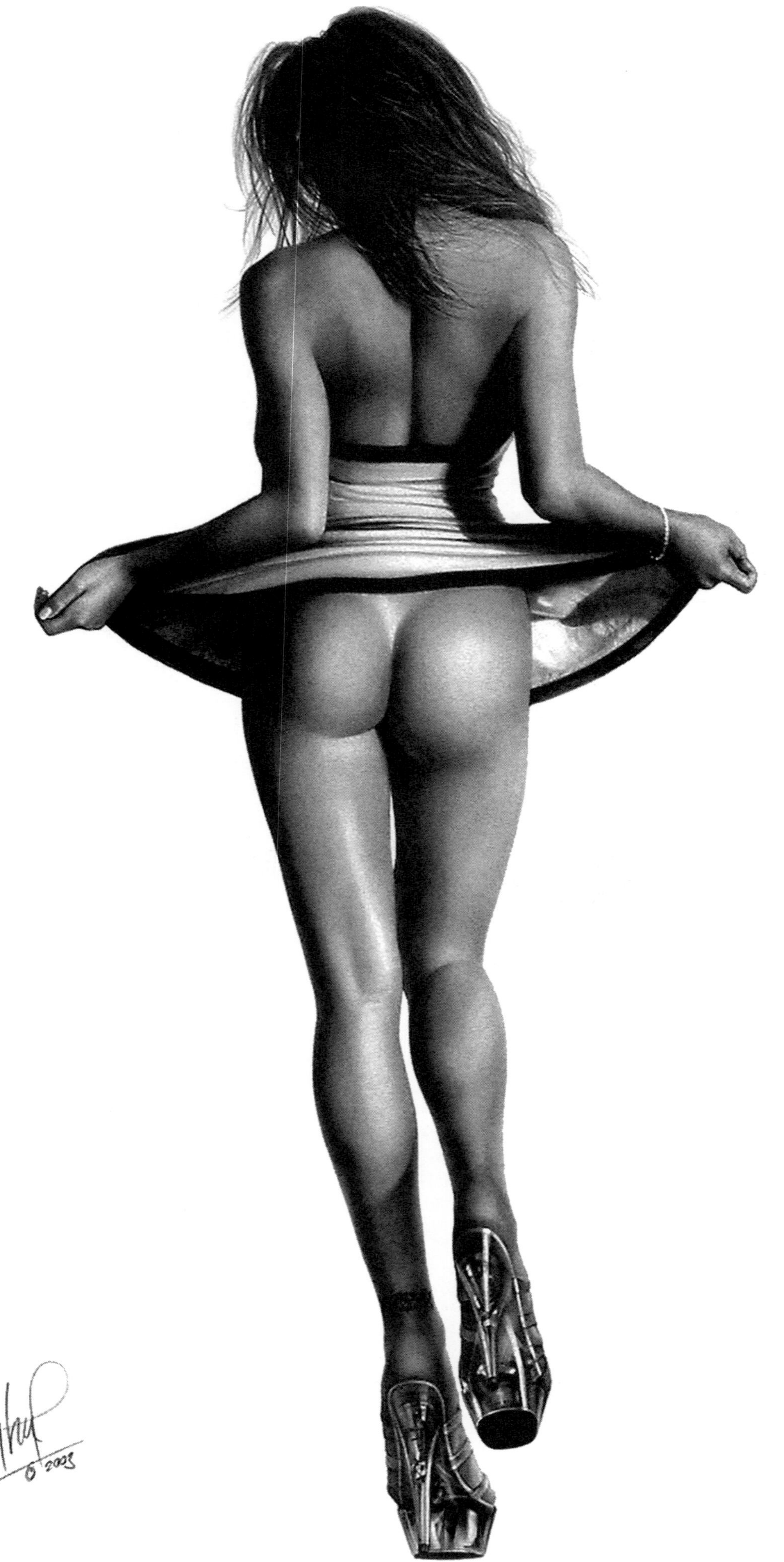

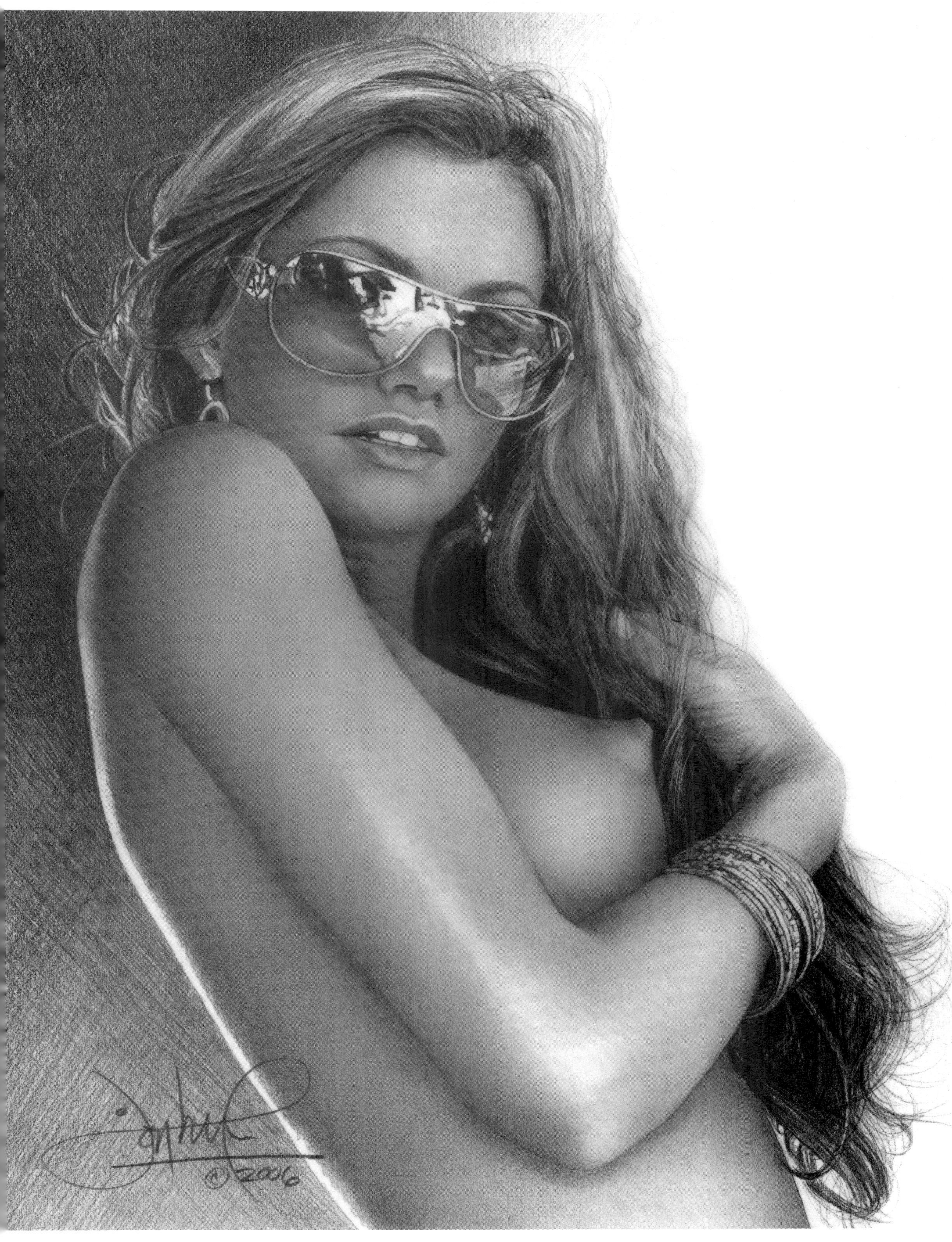
©2006

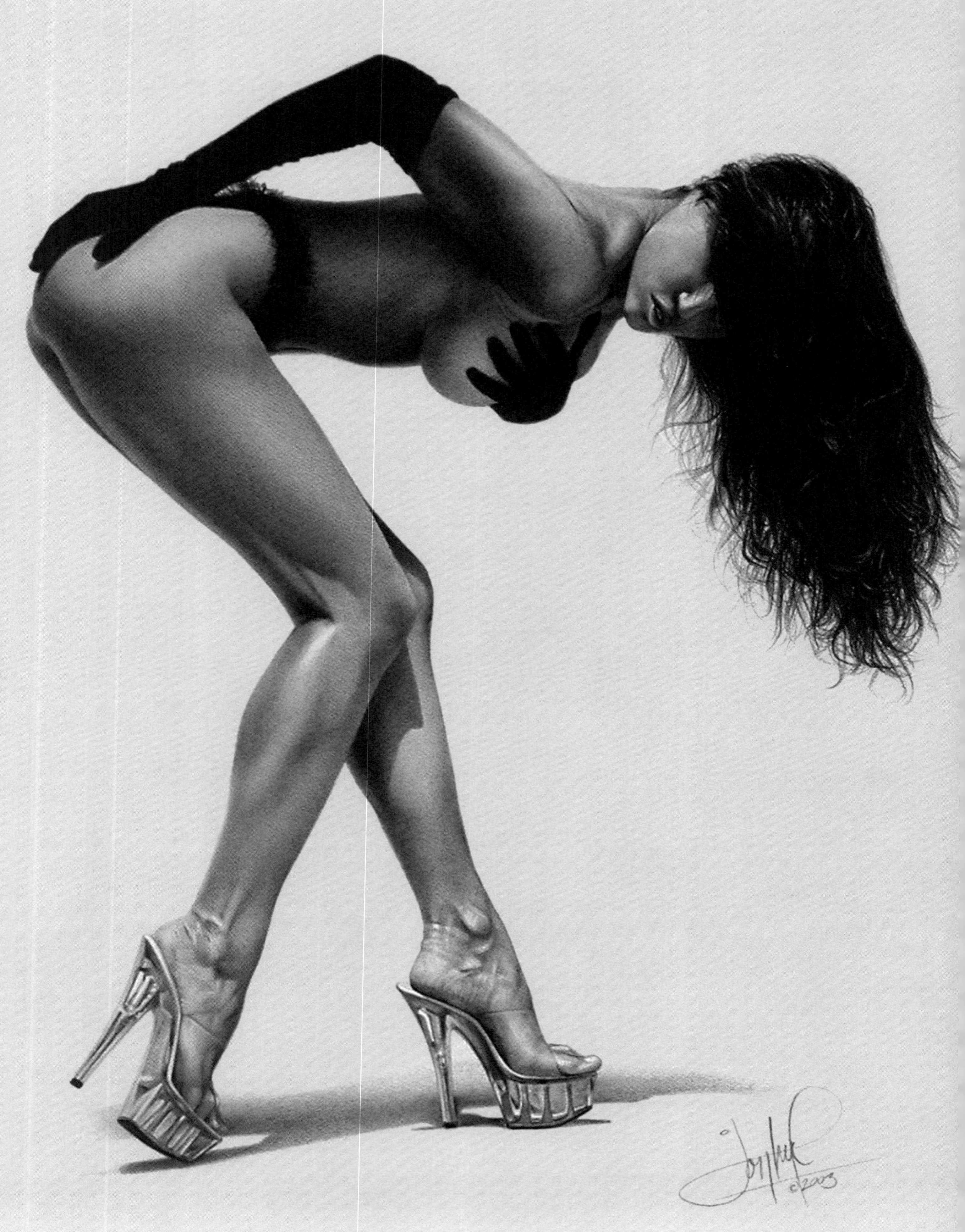
©2003

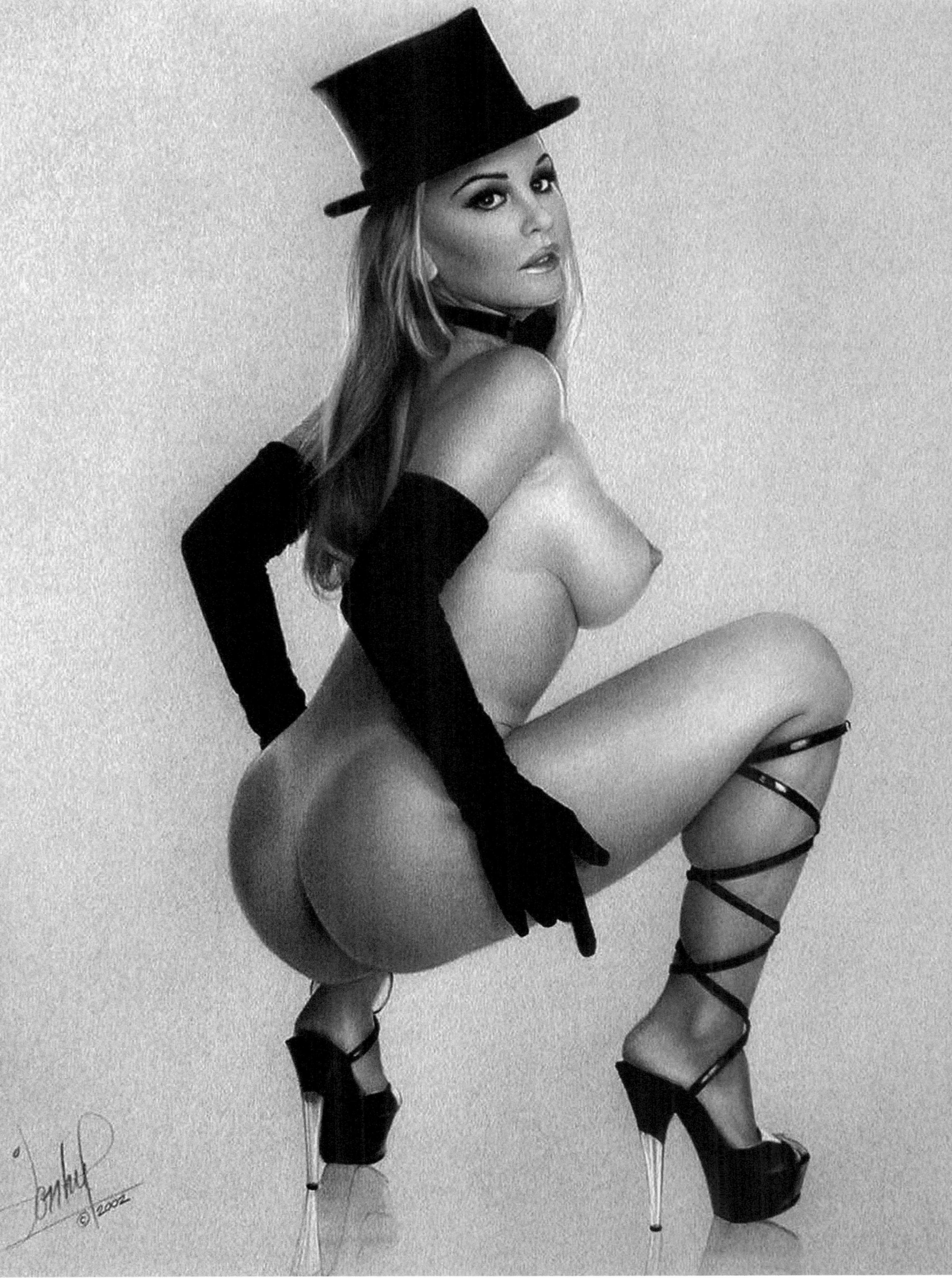
©2002

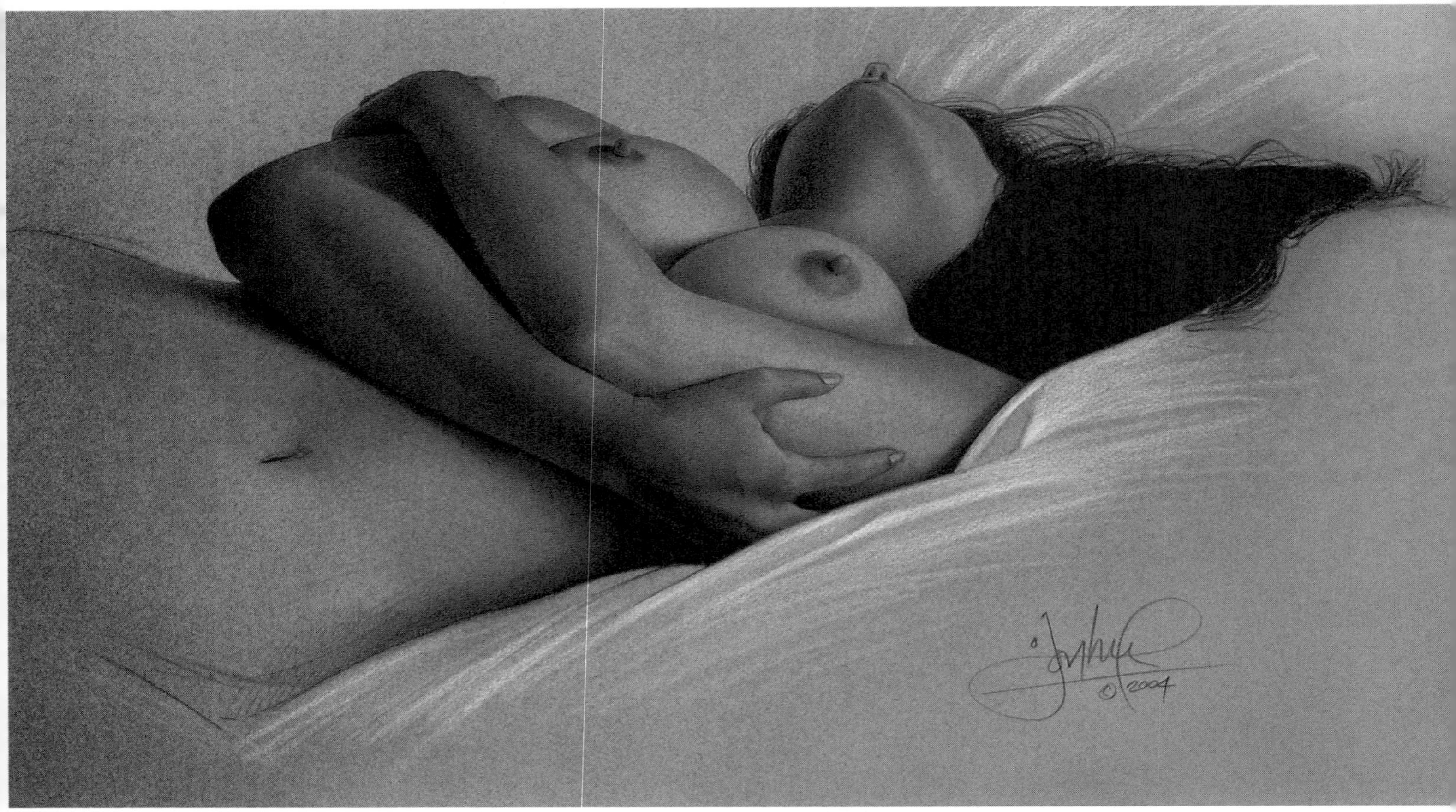

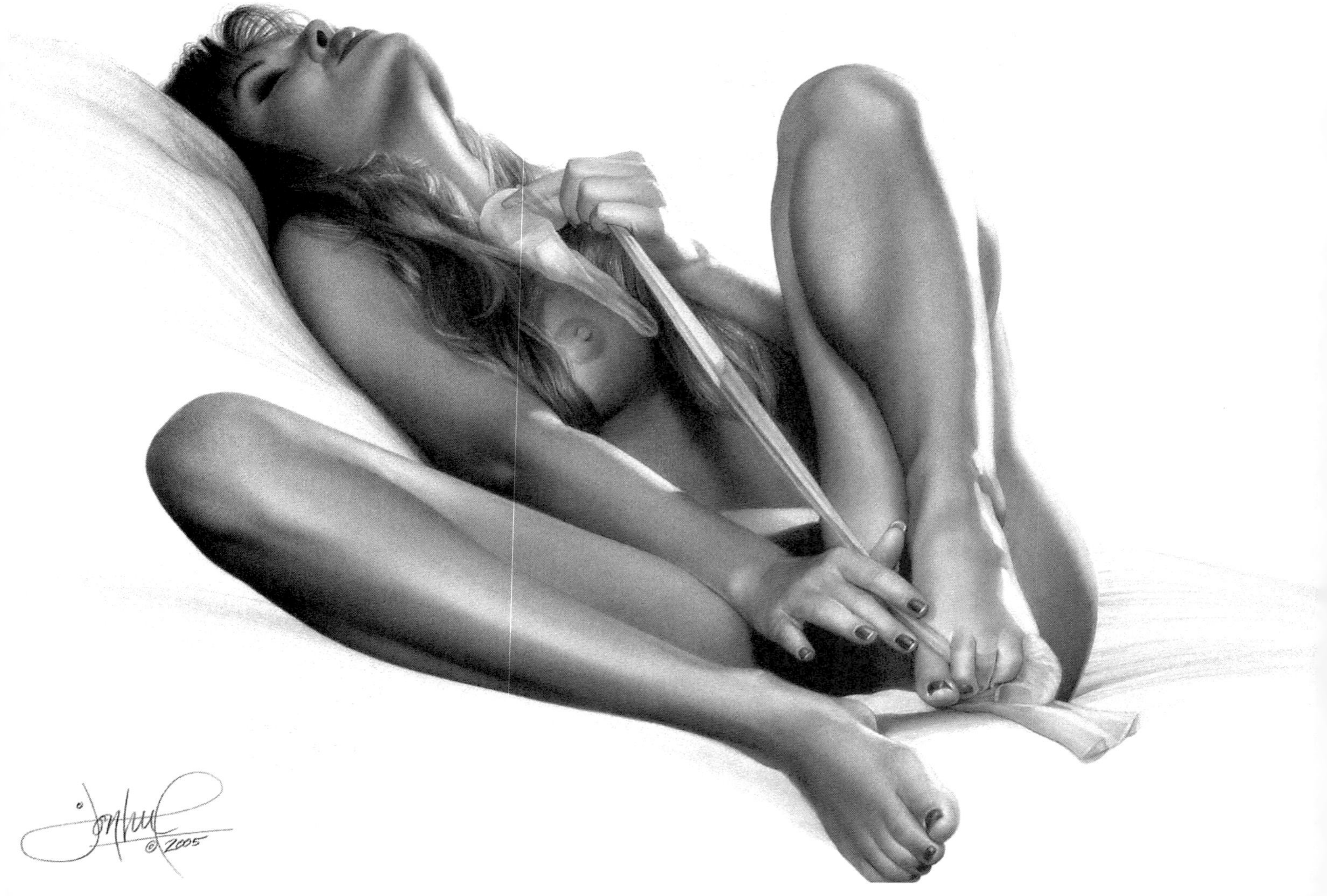

© 2004

© 2005

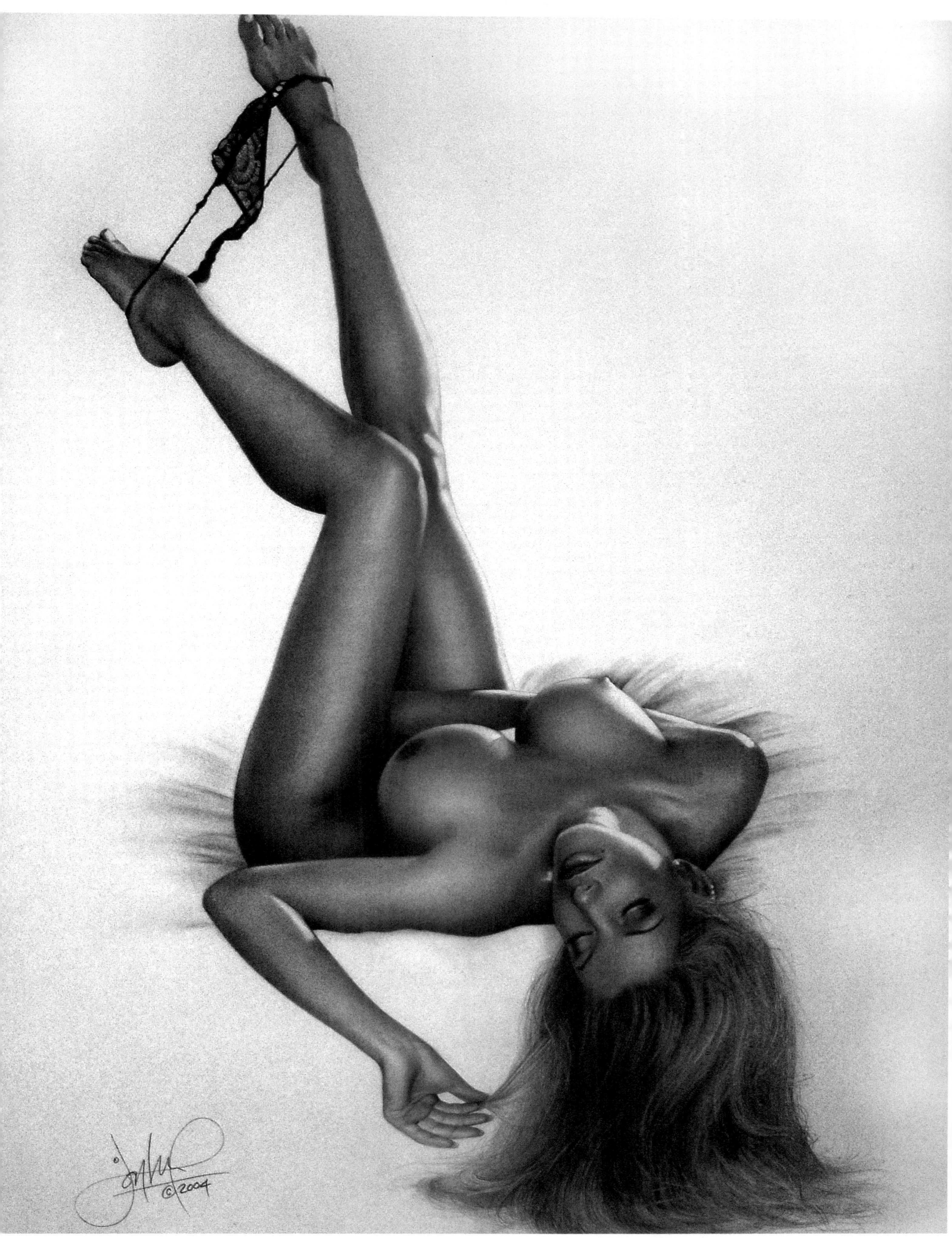
©2004

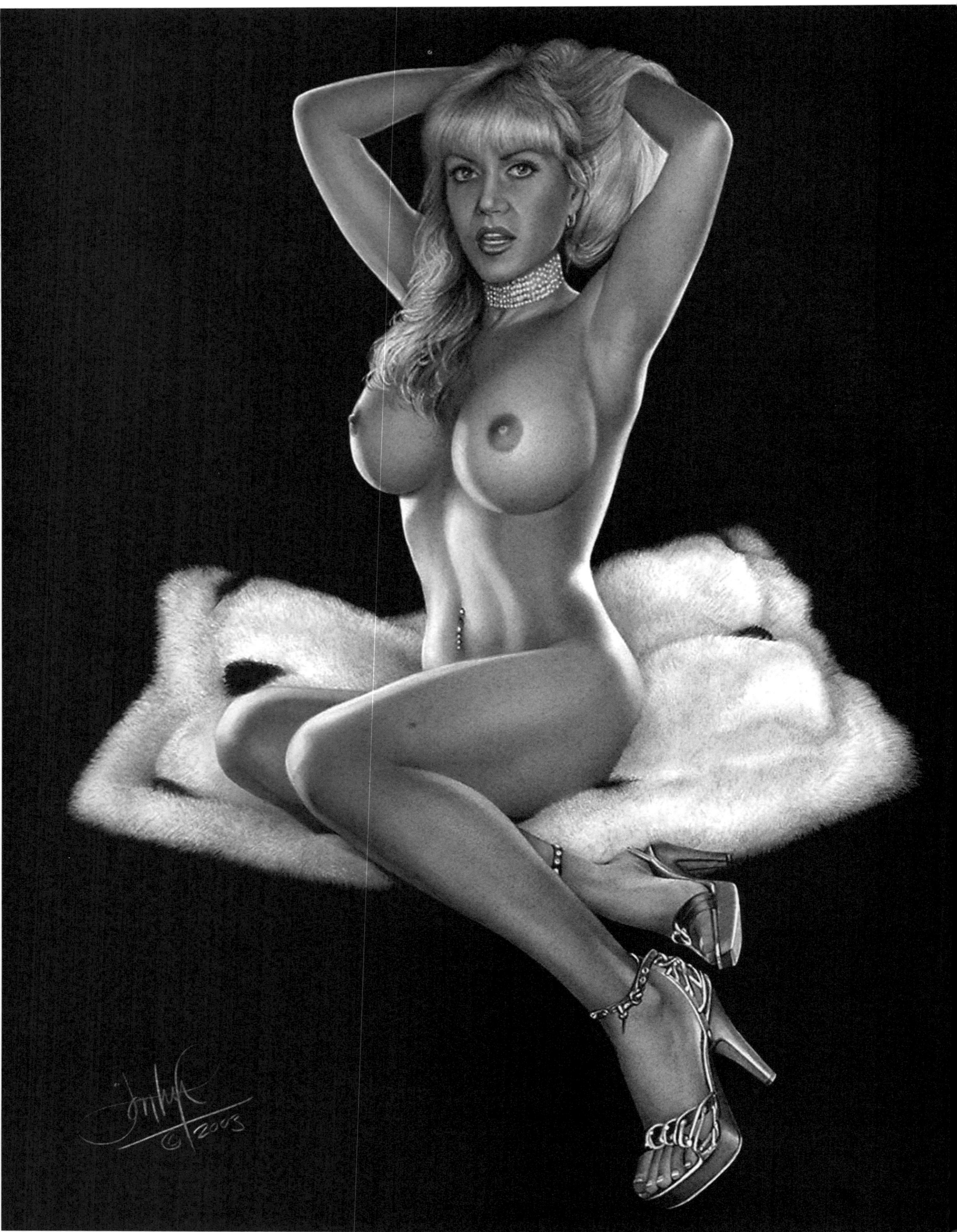

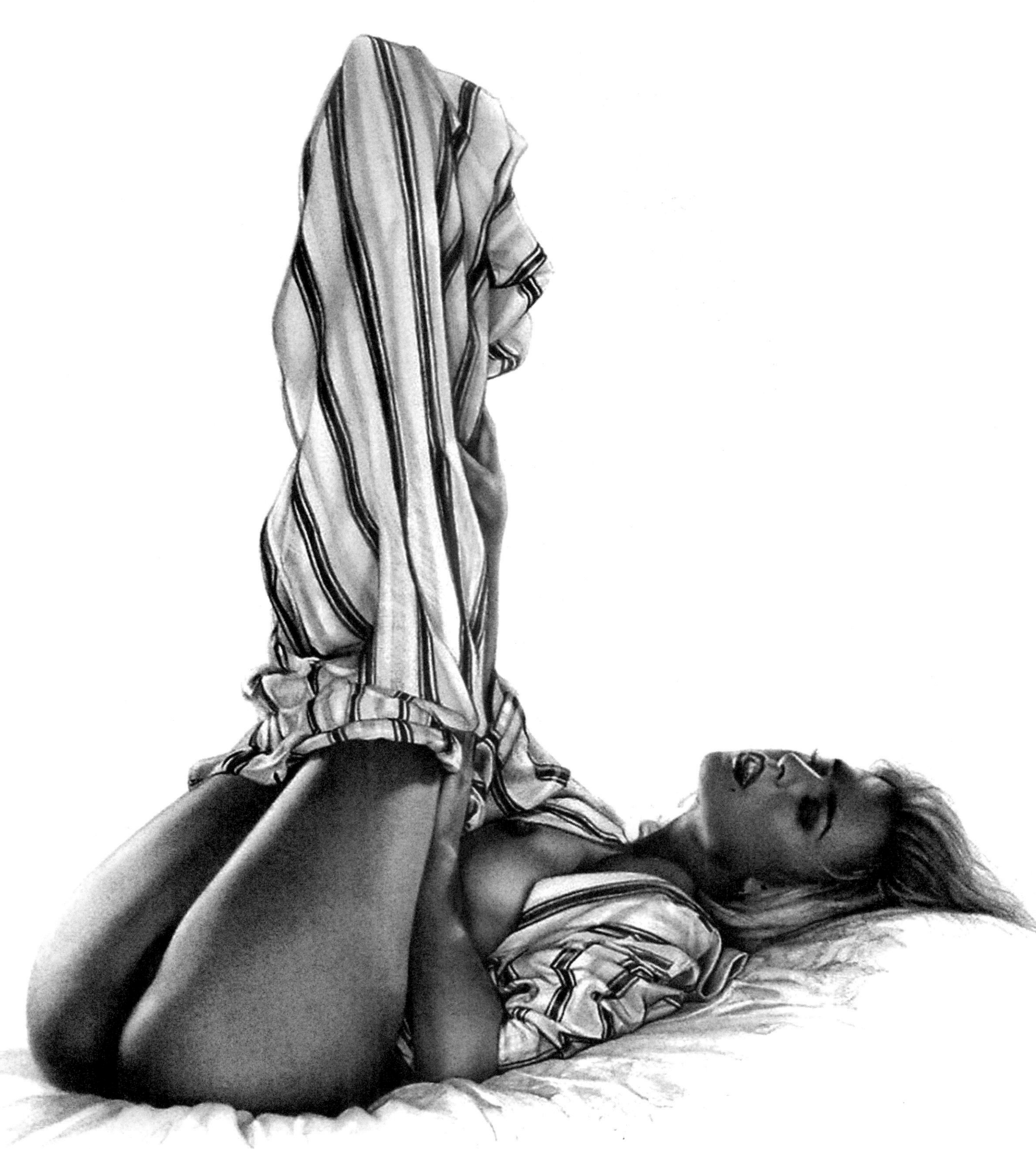
©2003

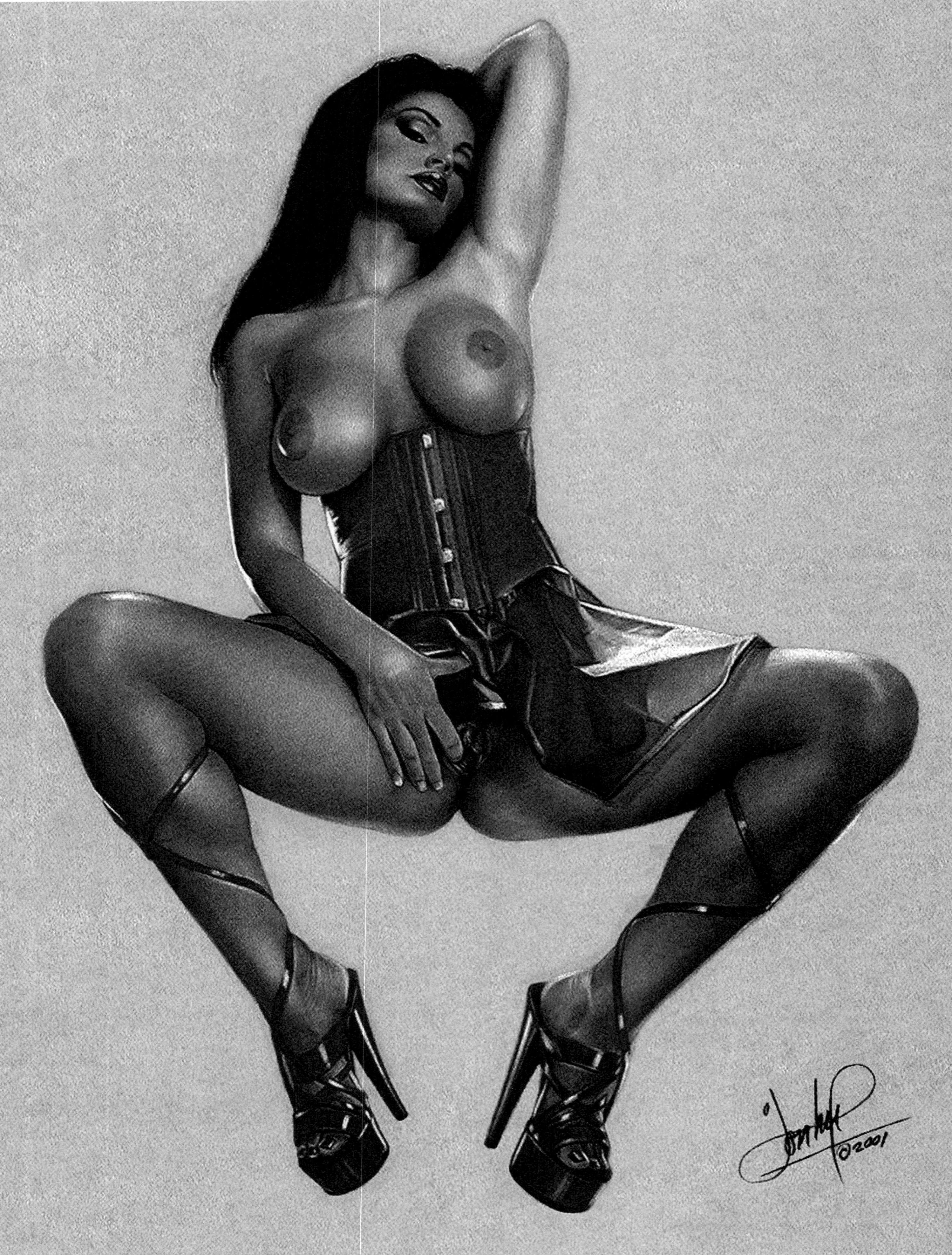
©2001

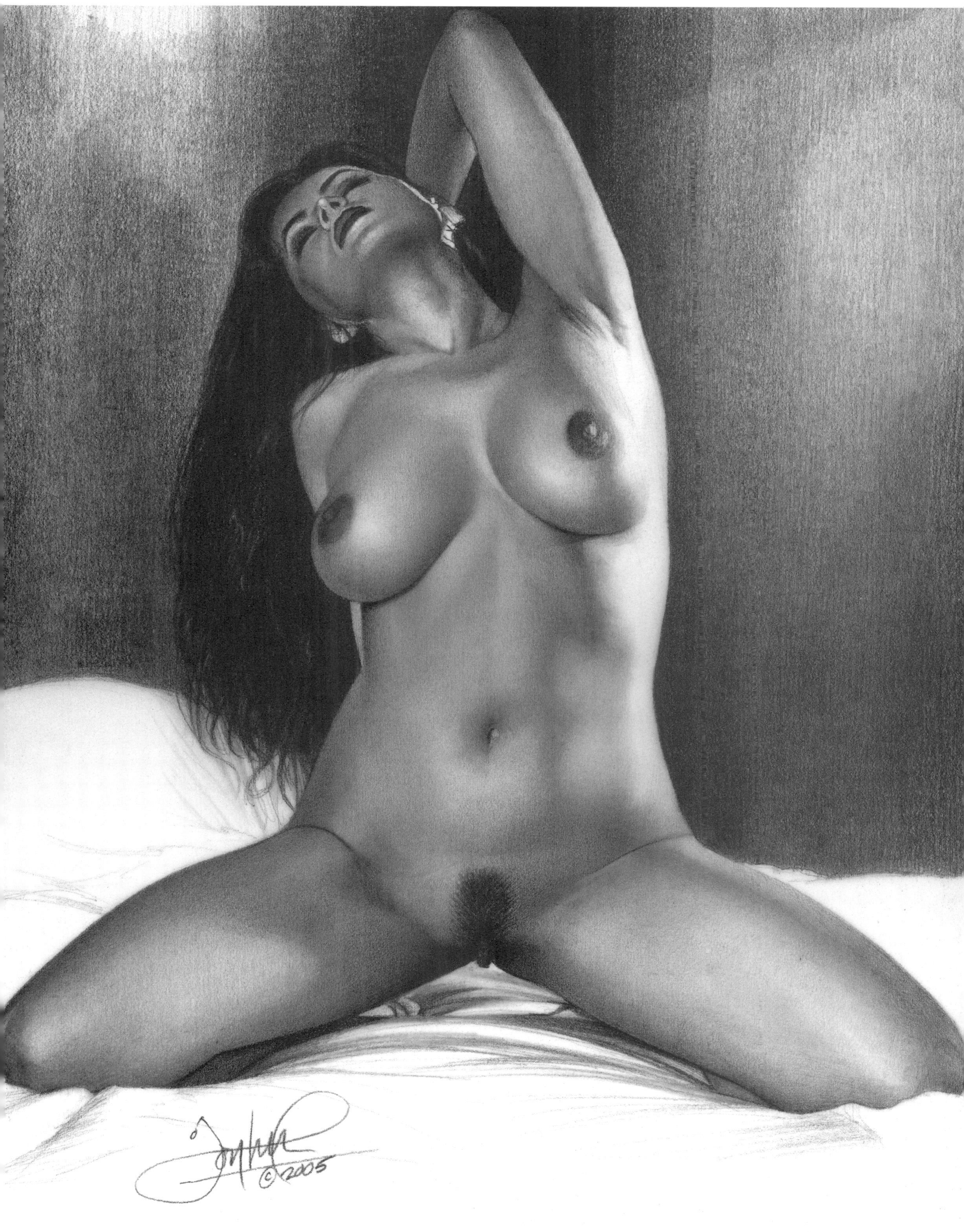
©2005

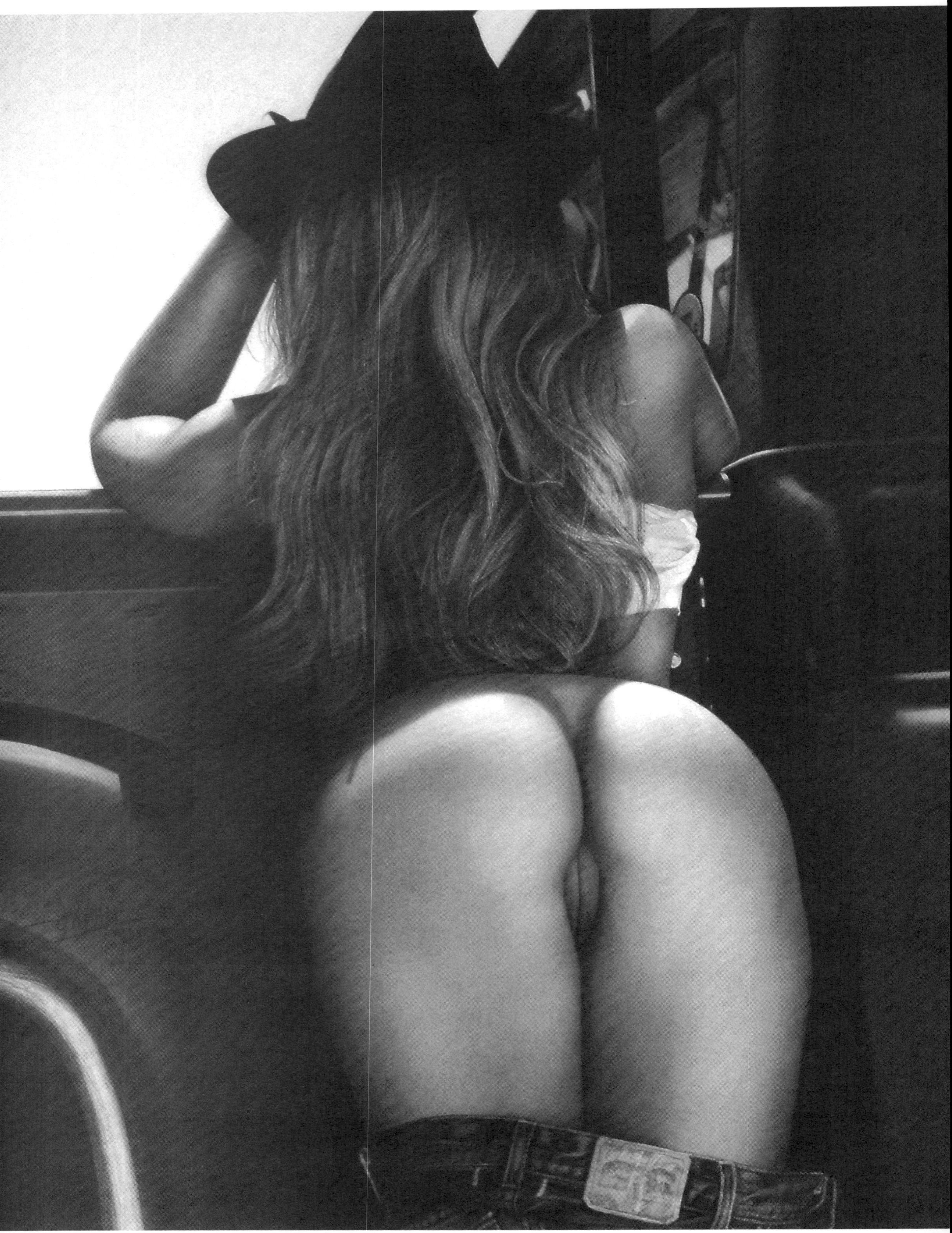

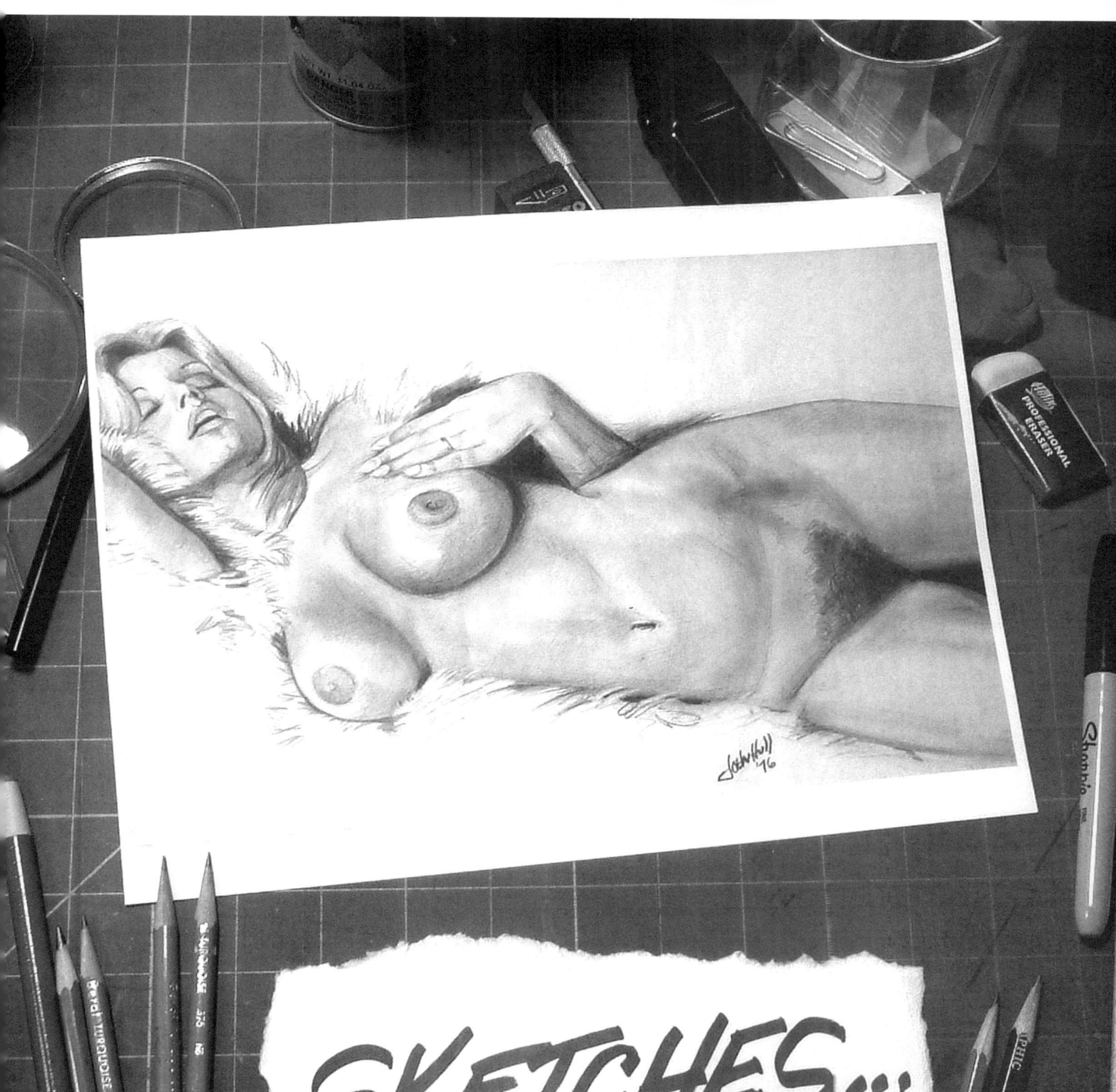

SKETCHES...

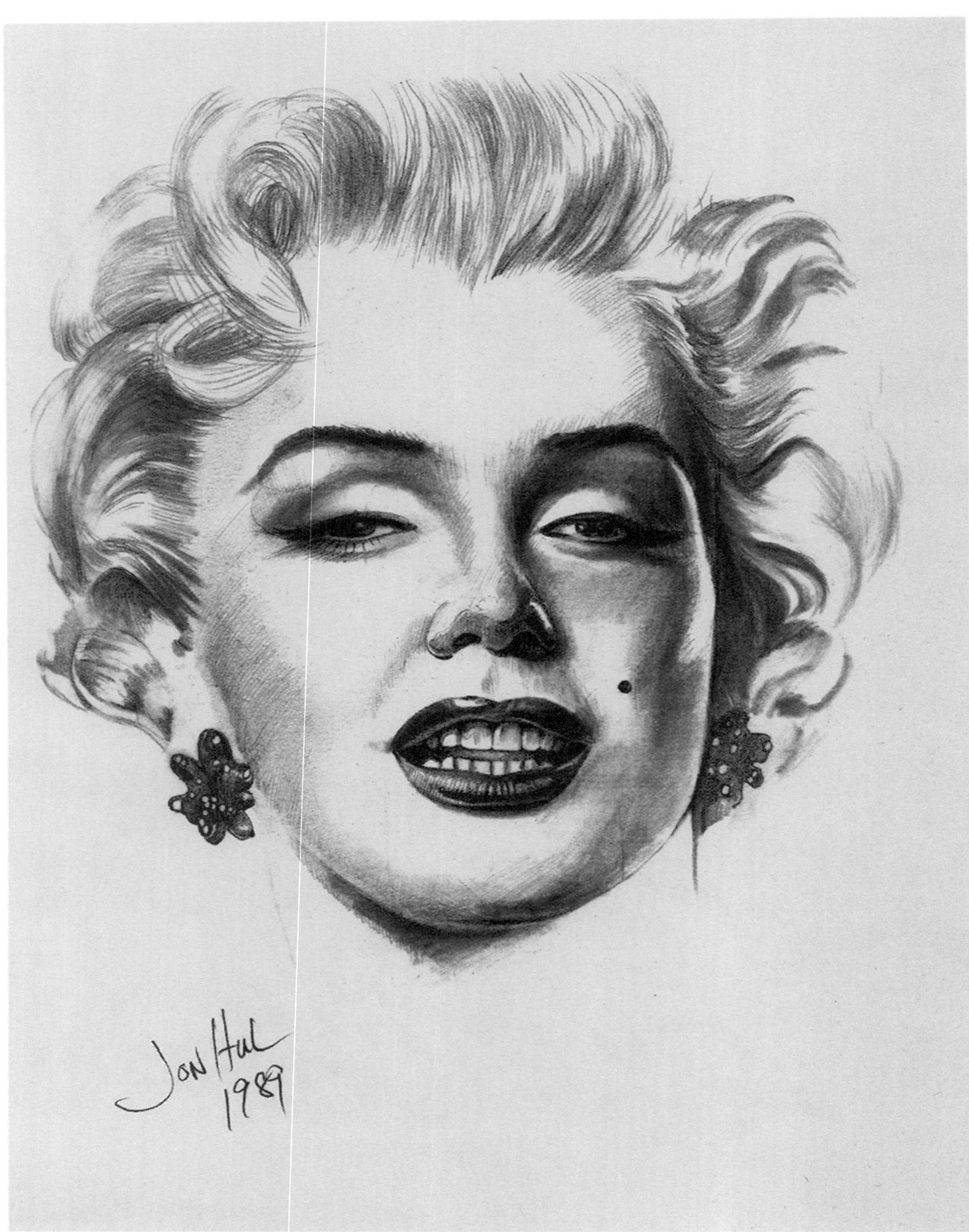
Jon Hul
1989

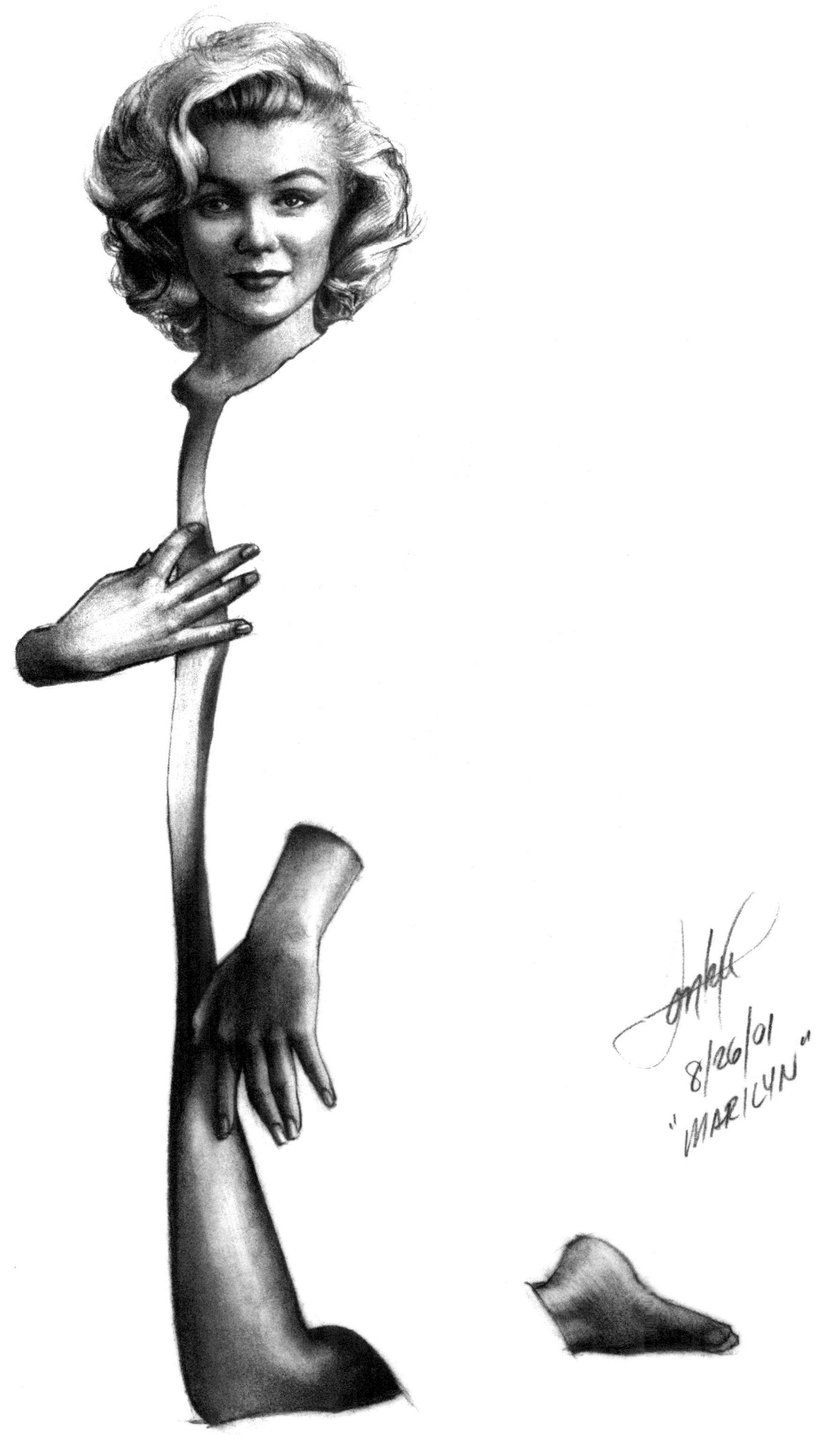
8/26/01
"MARILYN"

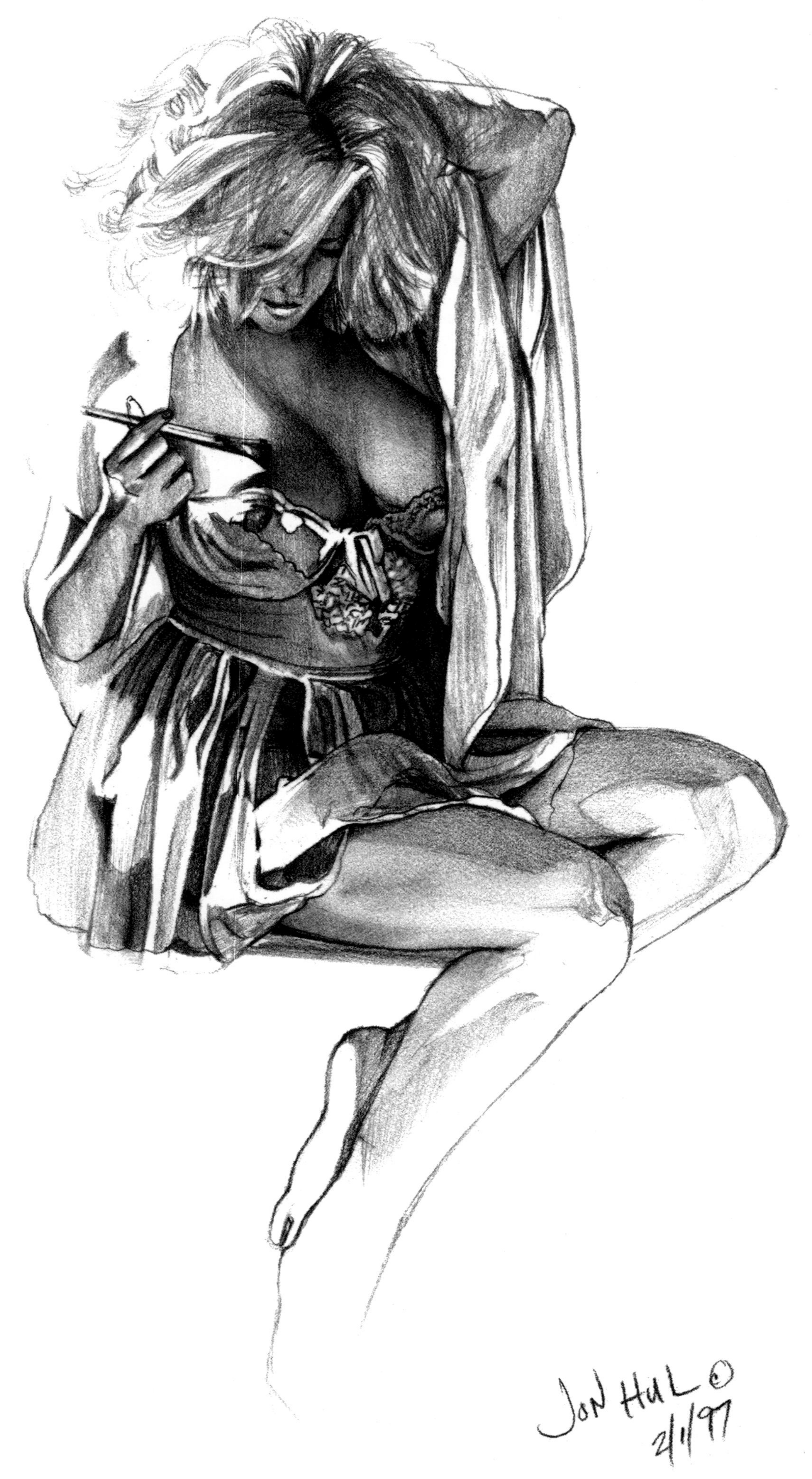
Jon Hul ©
2/1/97

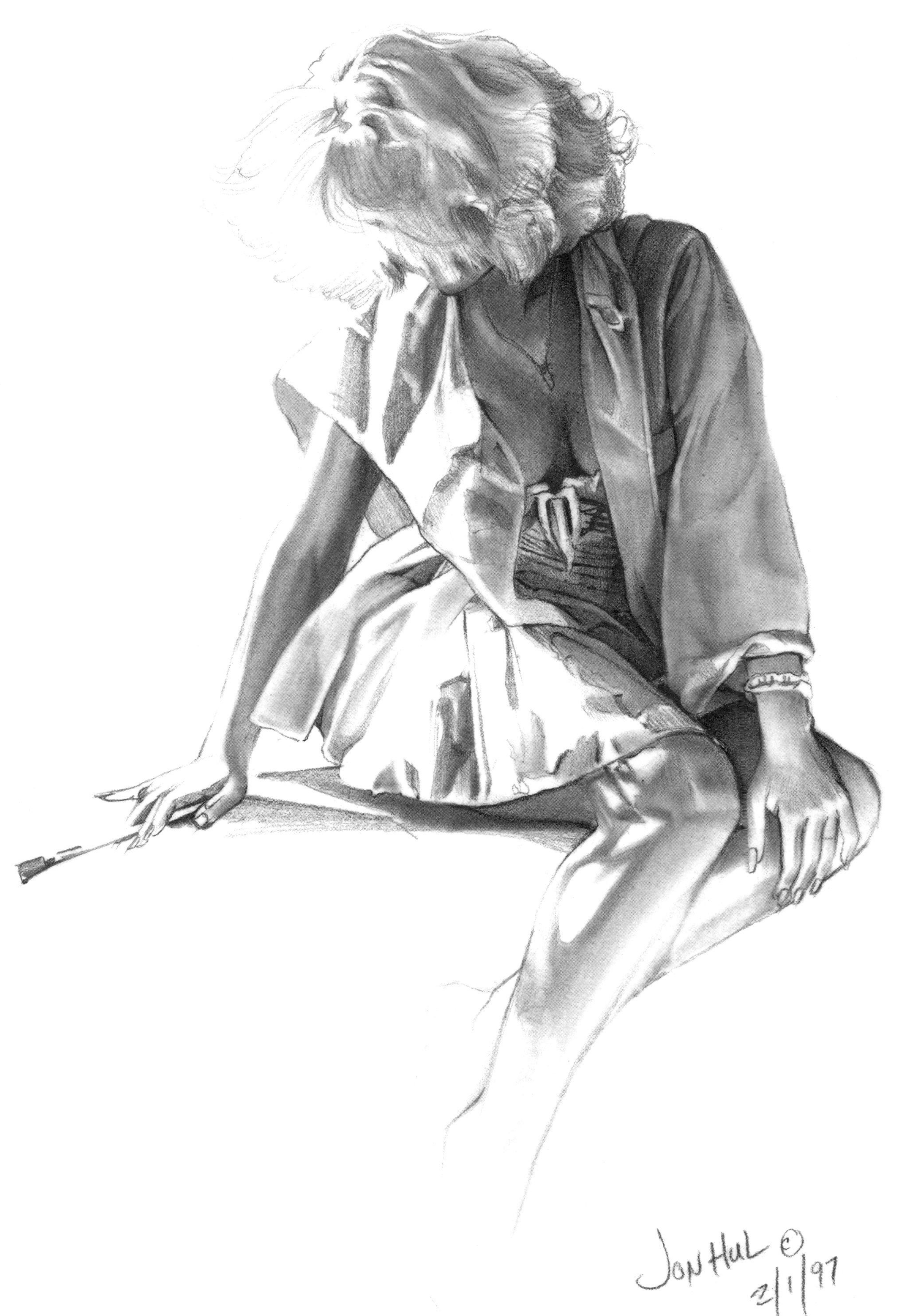
Jon Hul ©
2/1/97

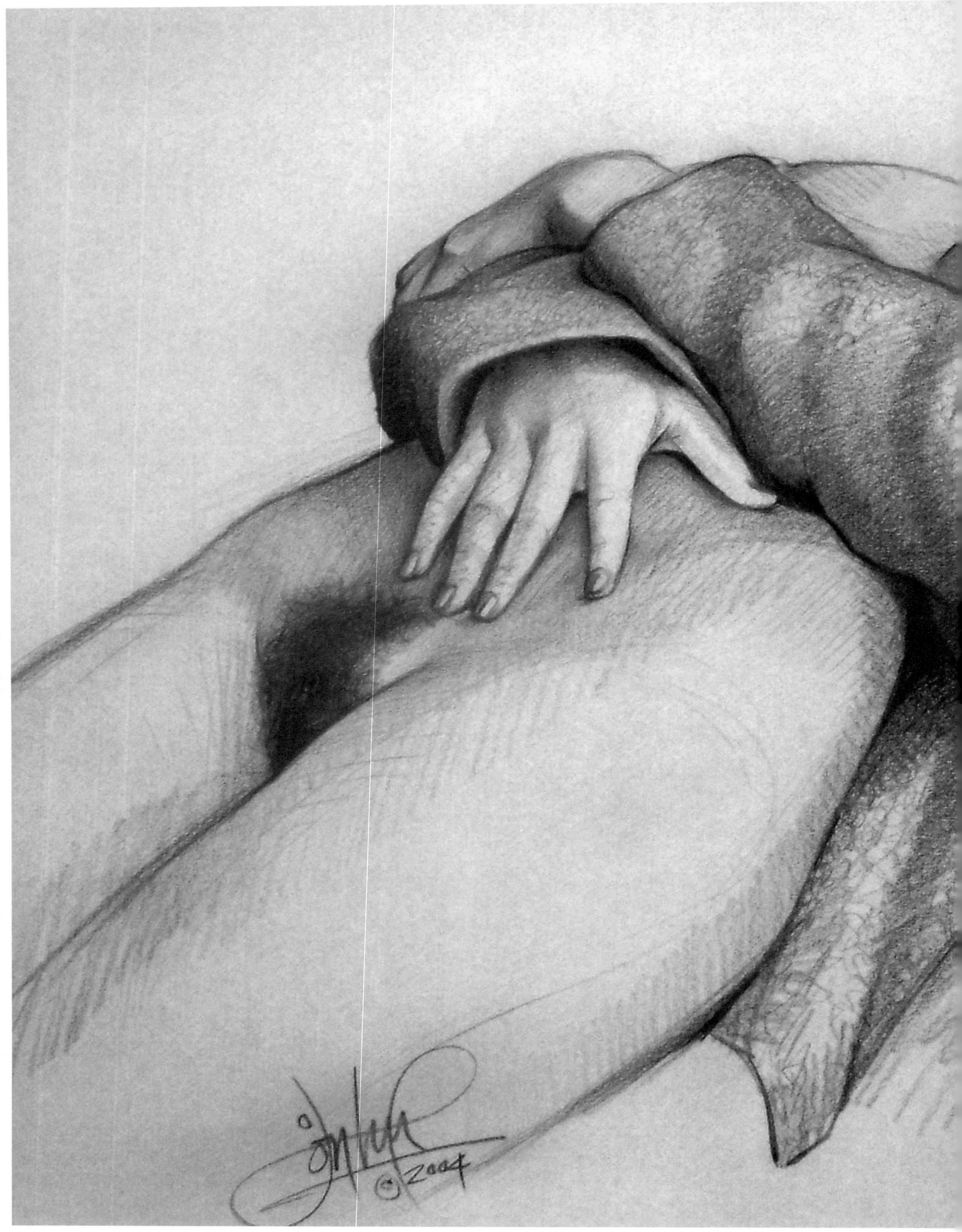
©2004

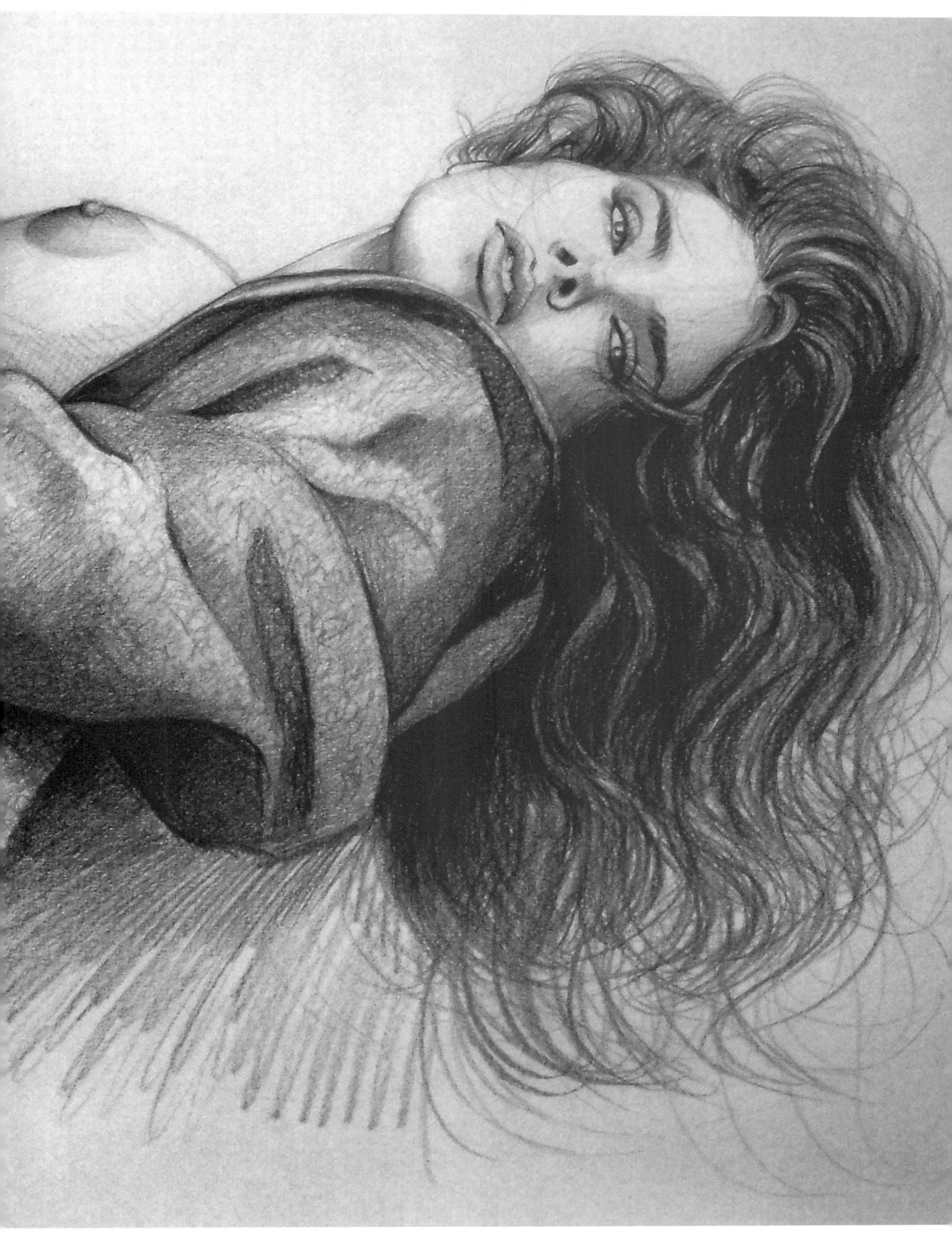

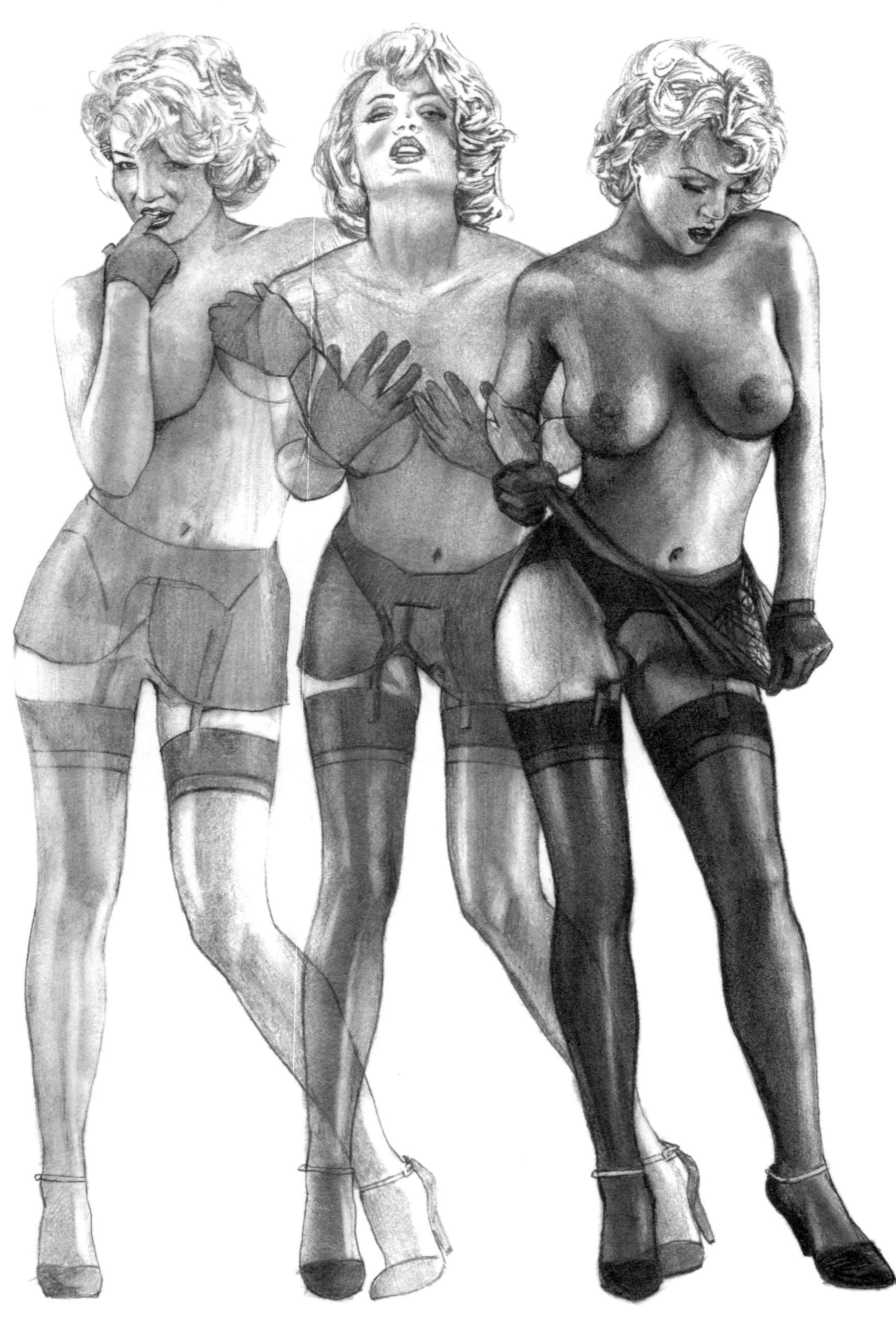

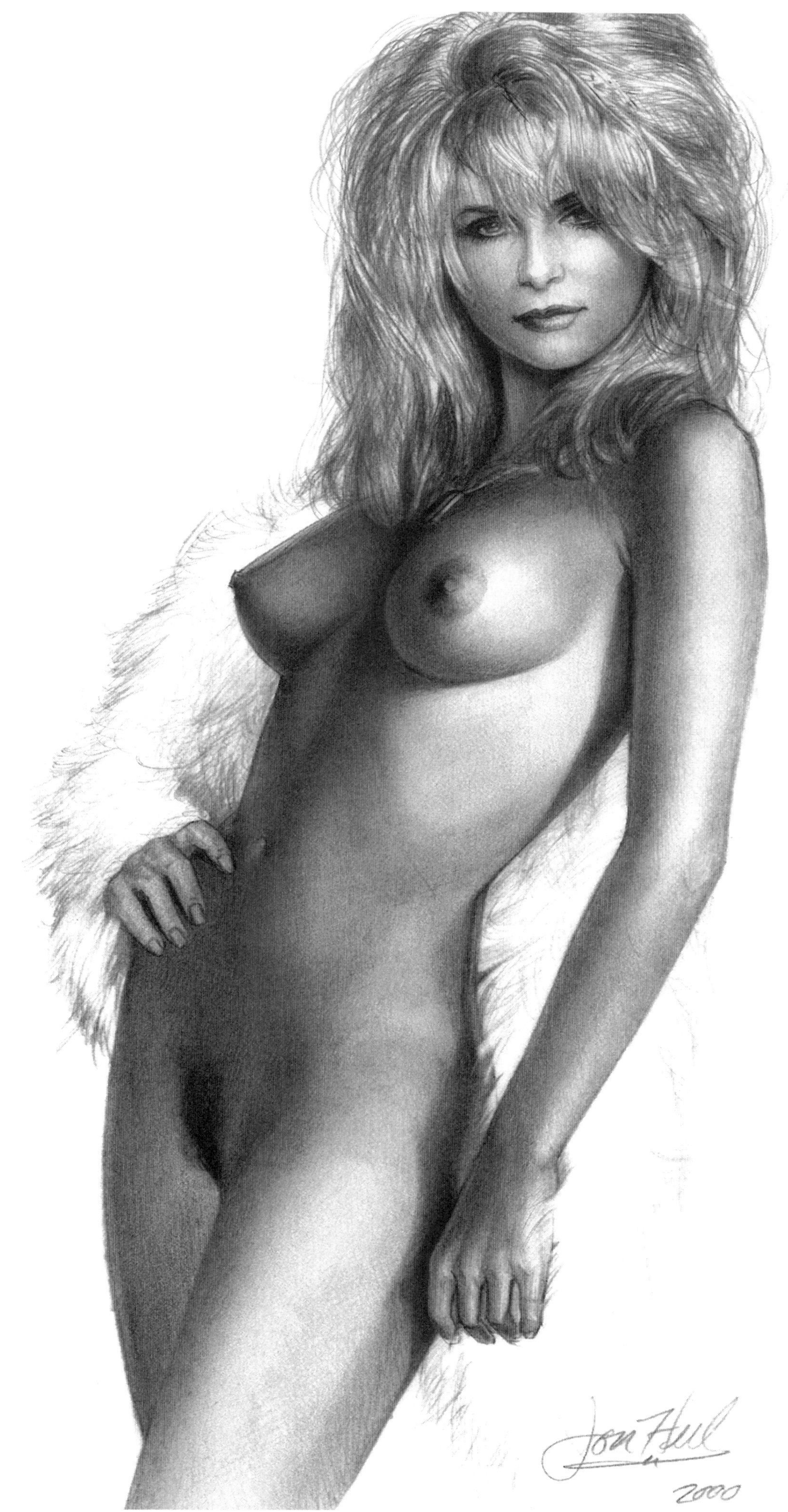
Jon Hul
2000

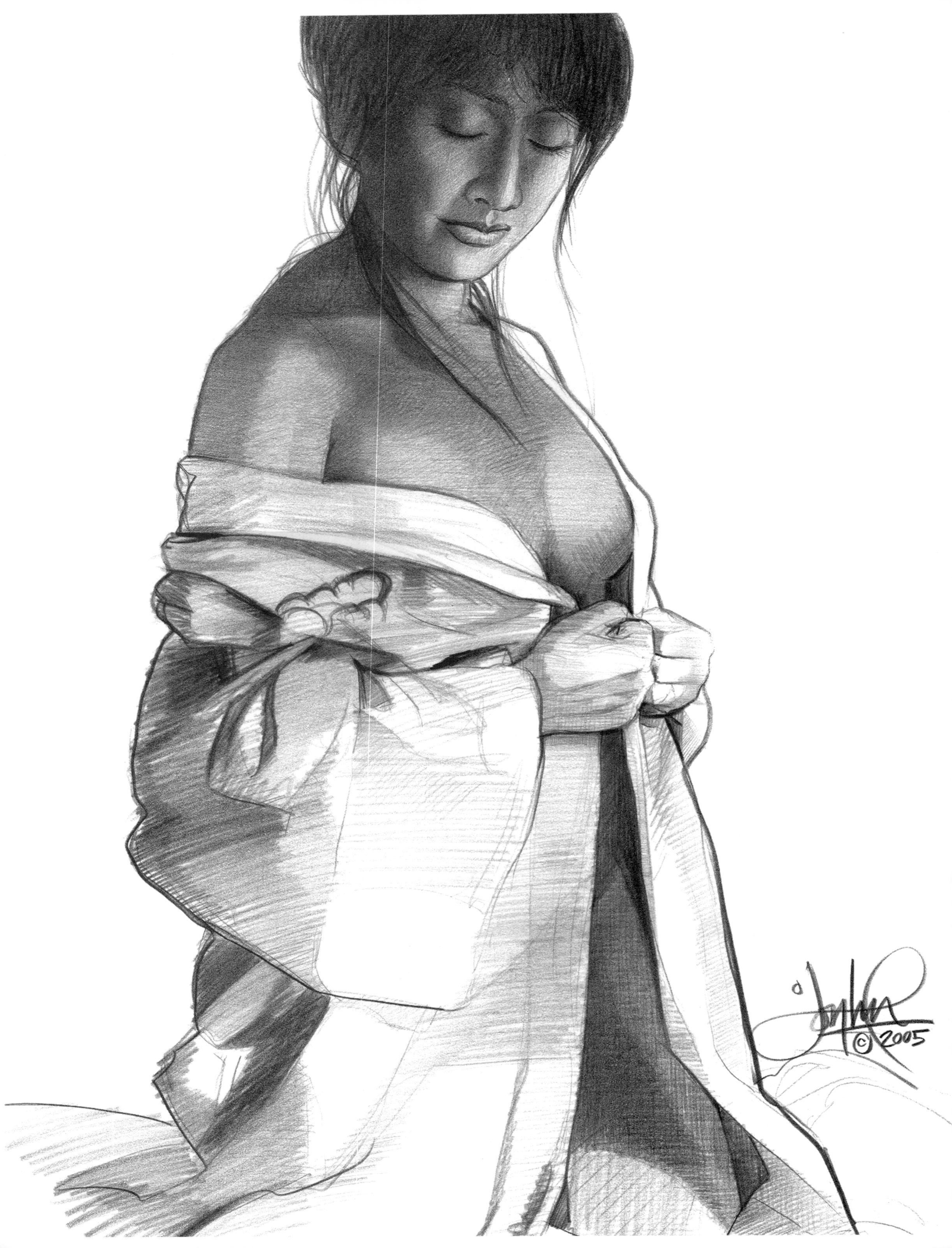
©2005

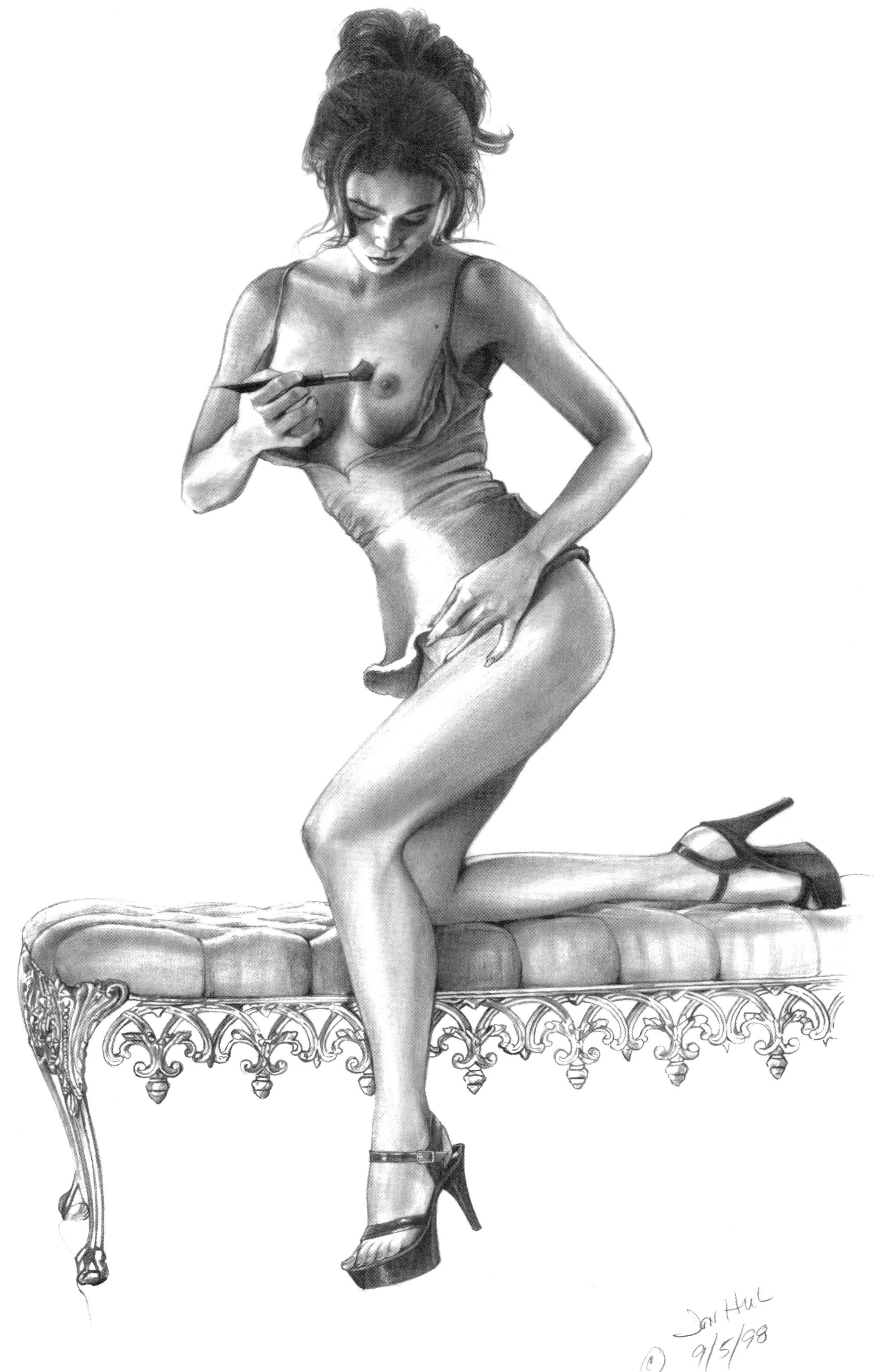
© 9/5/98

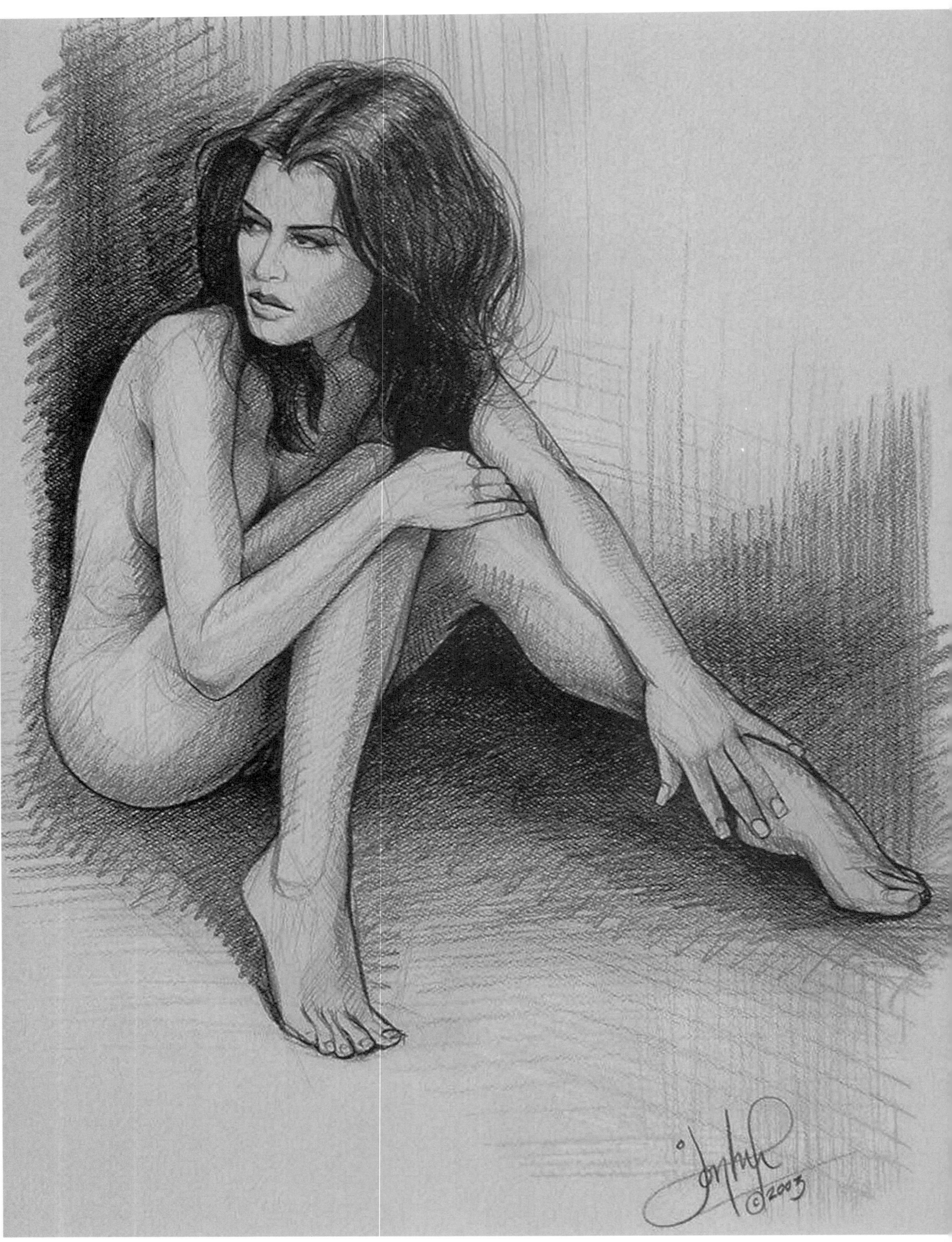
©2003

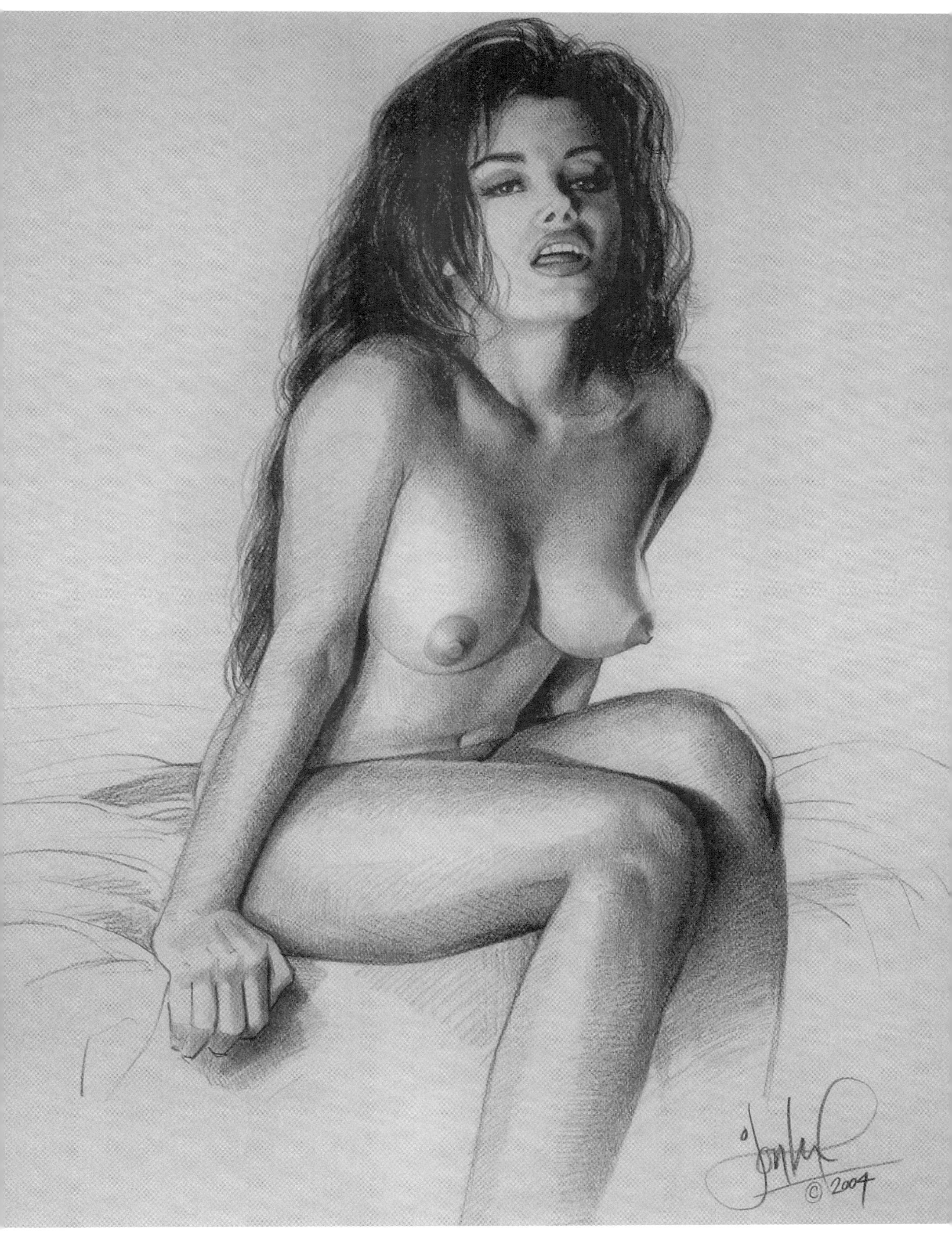
© 2004

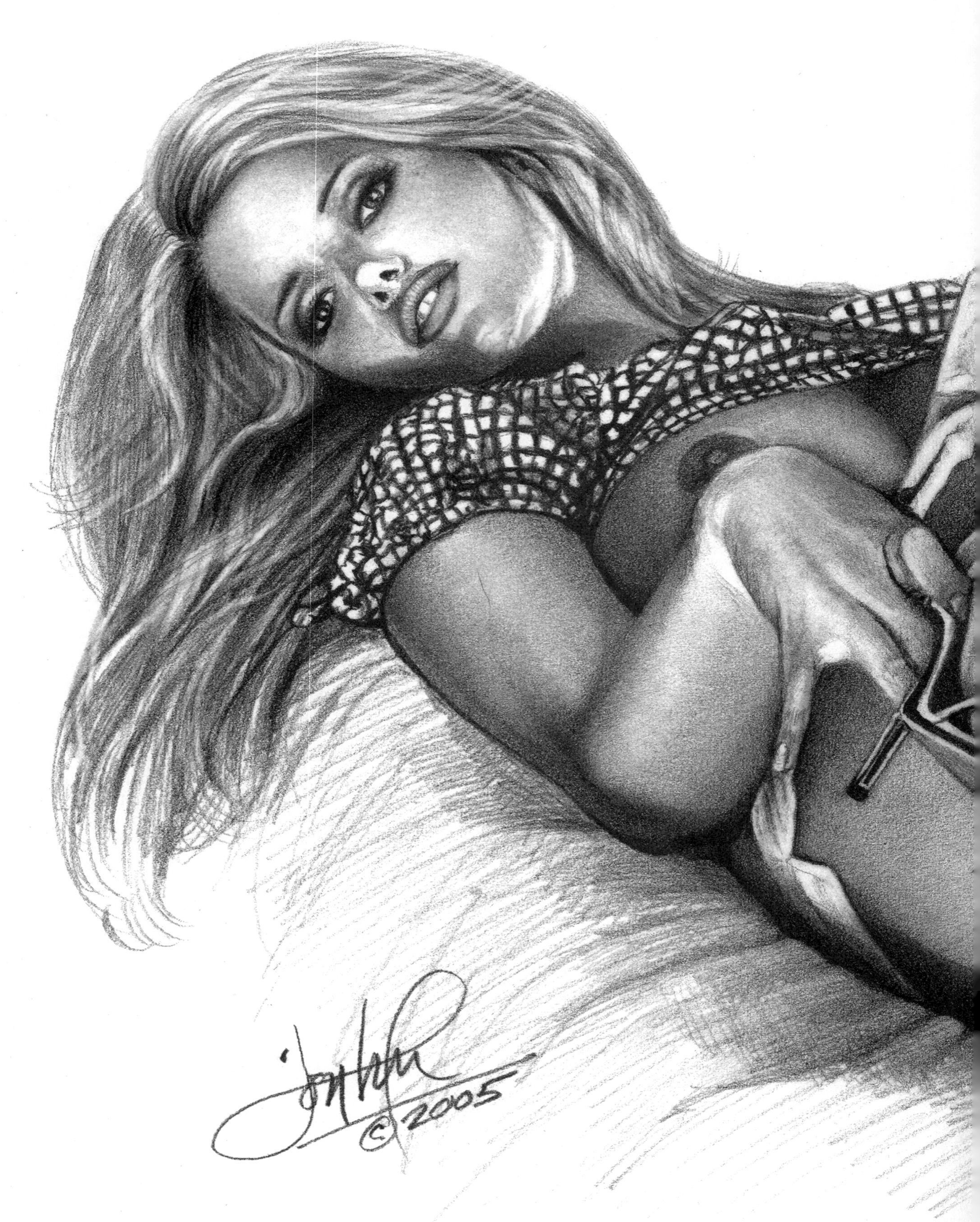
© 2005

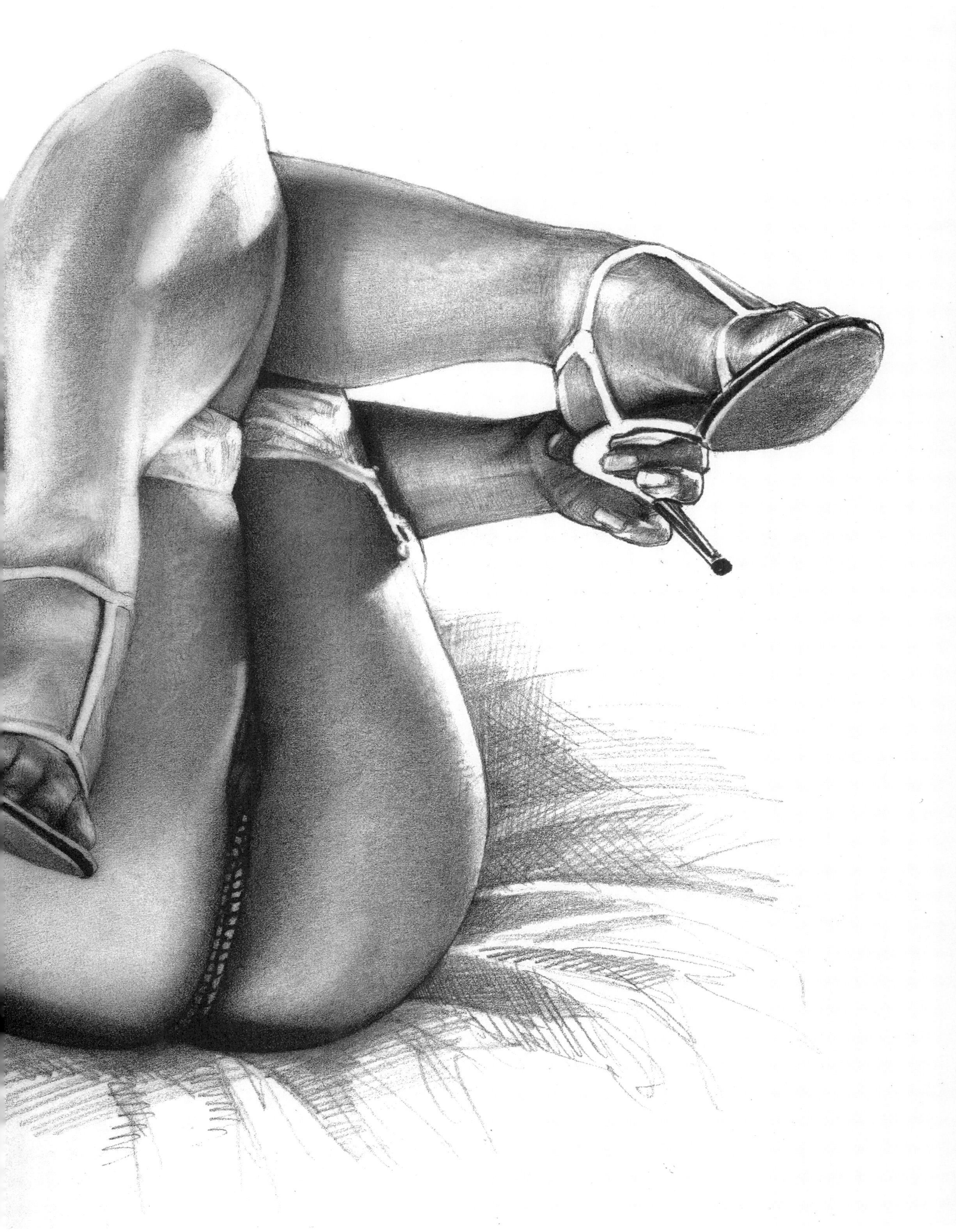

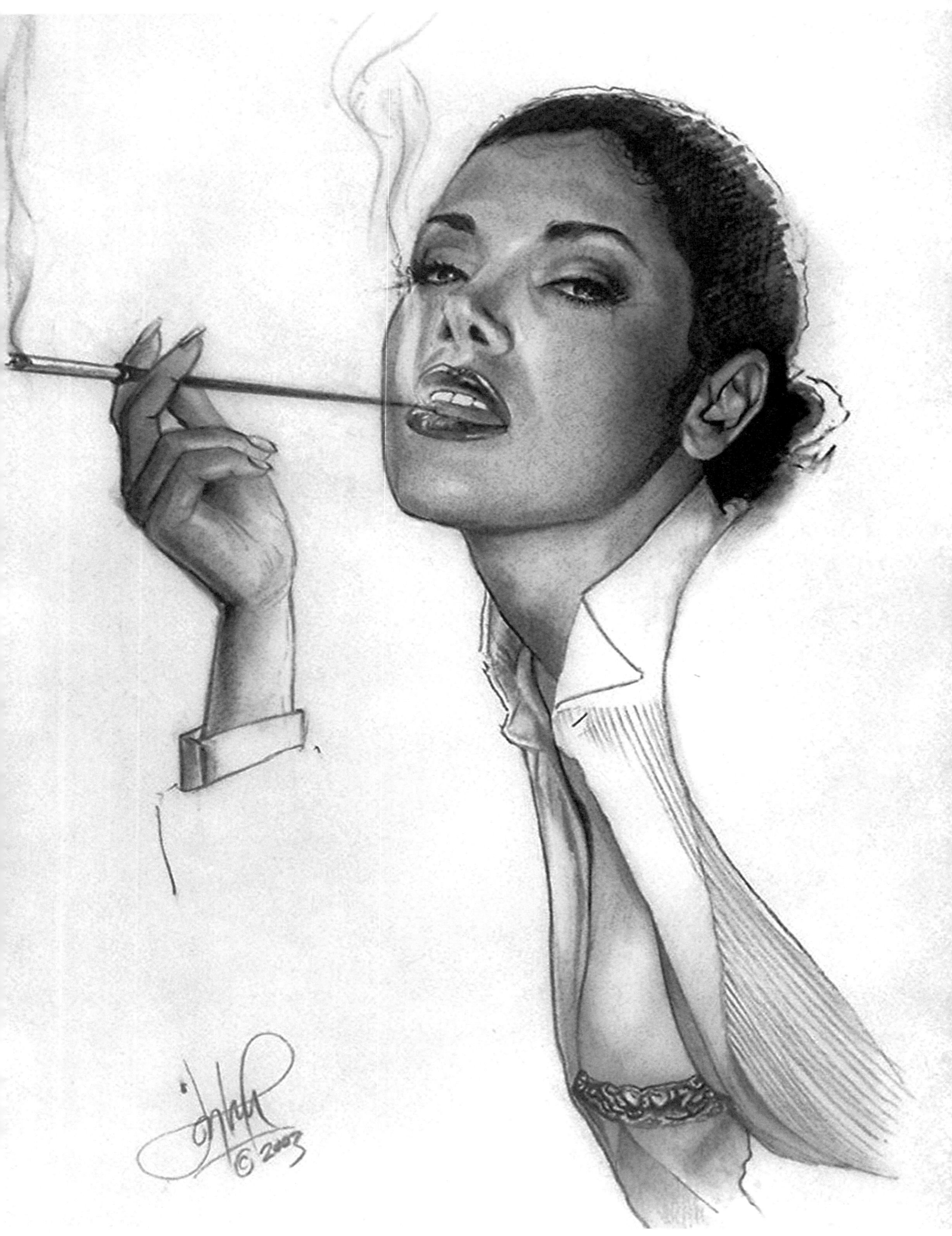

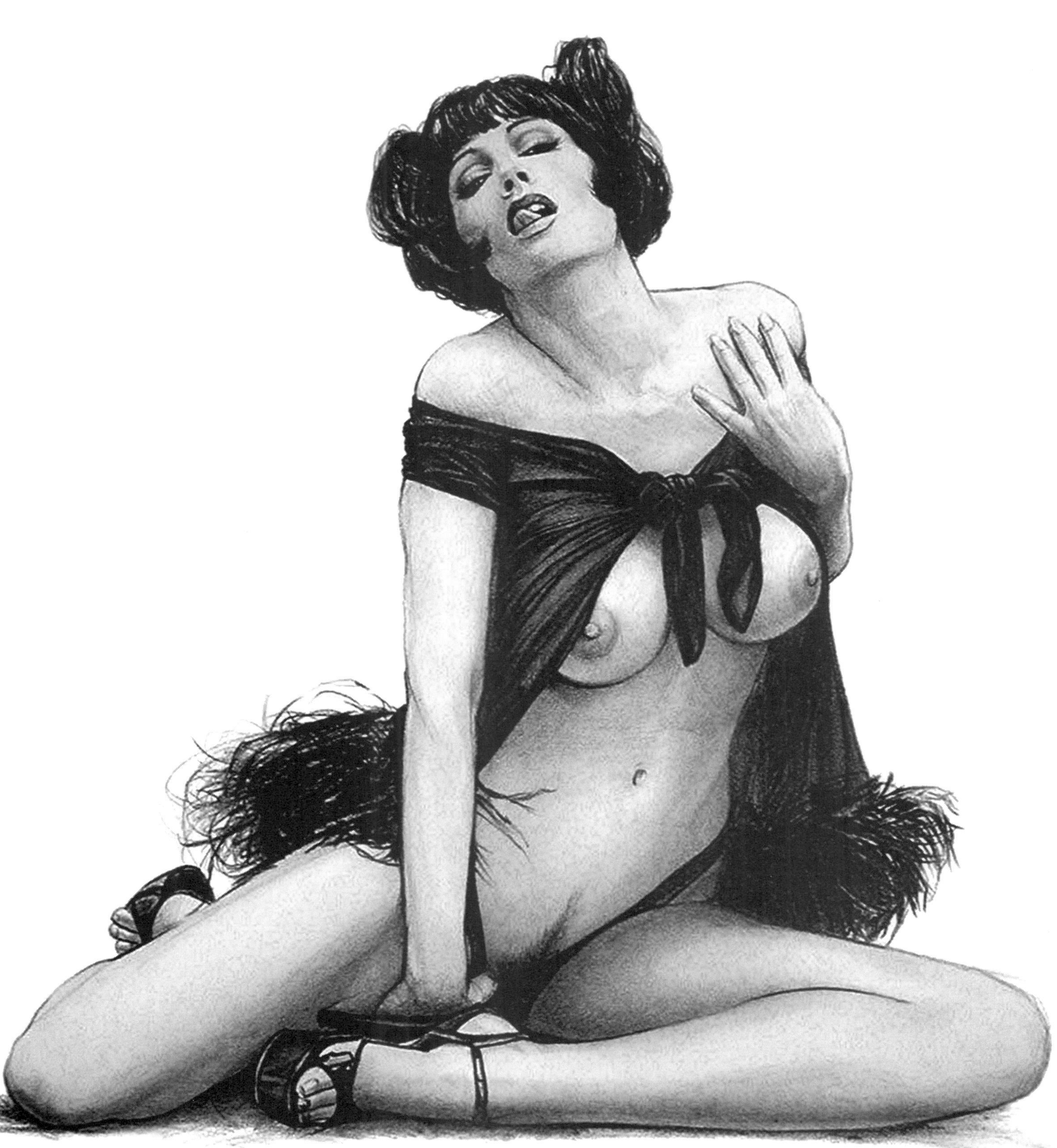
2001

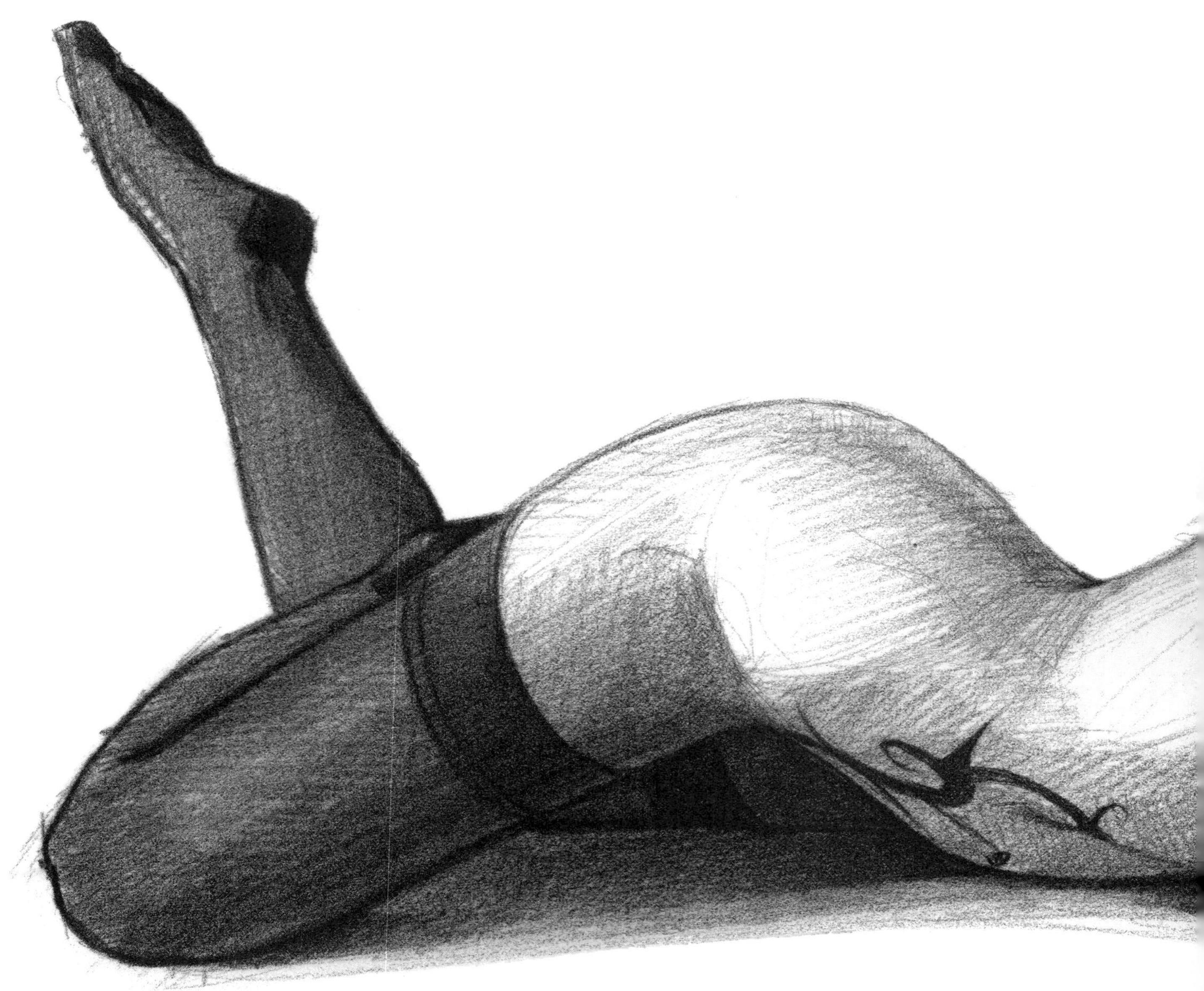

"Study"!

© 07/7 2005

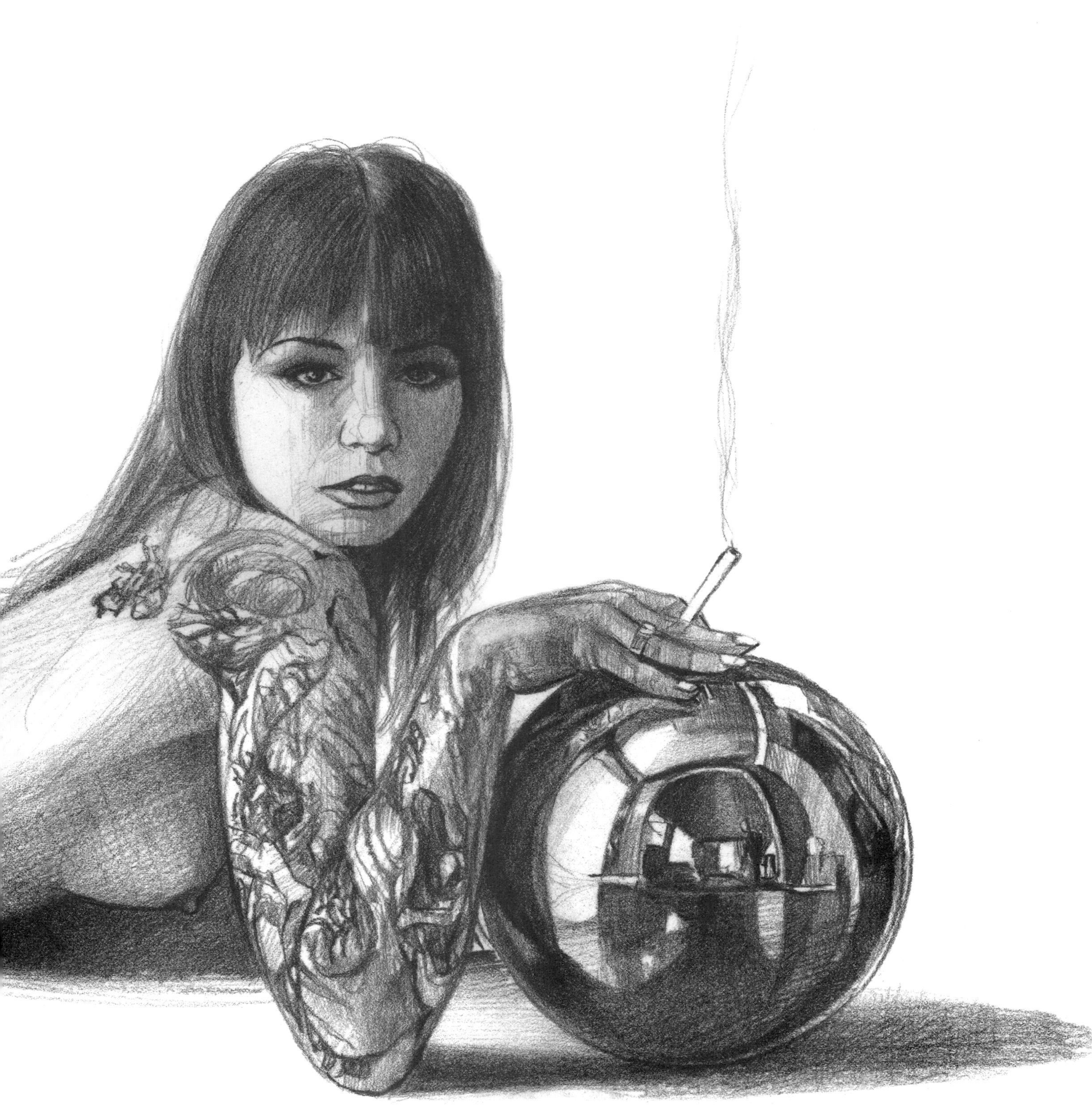

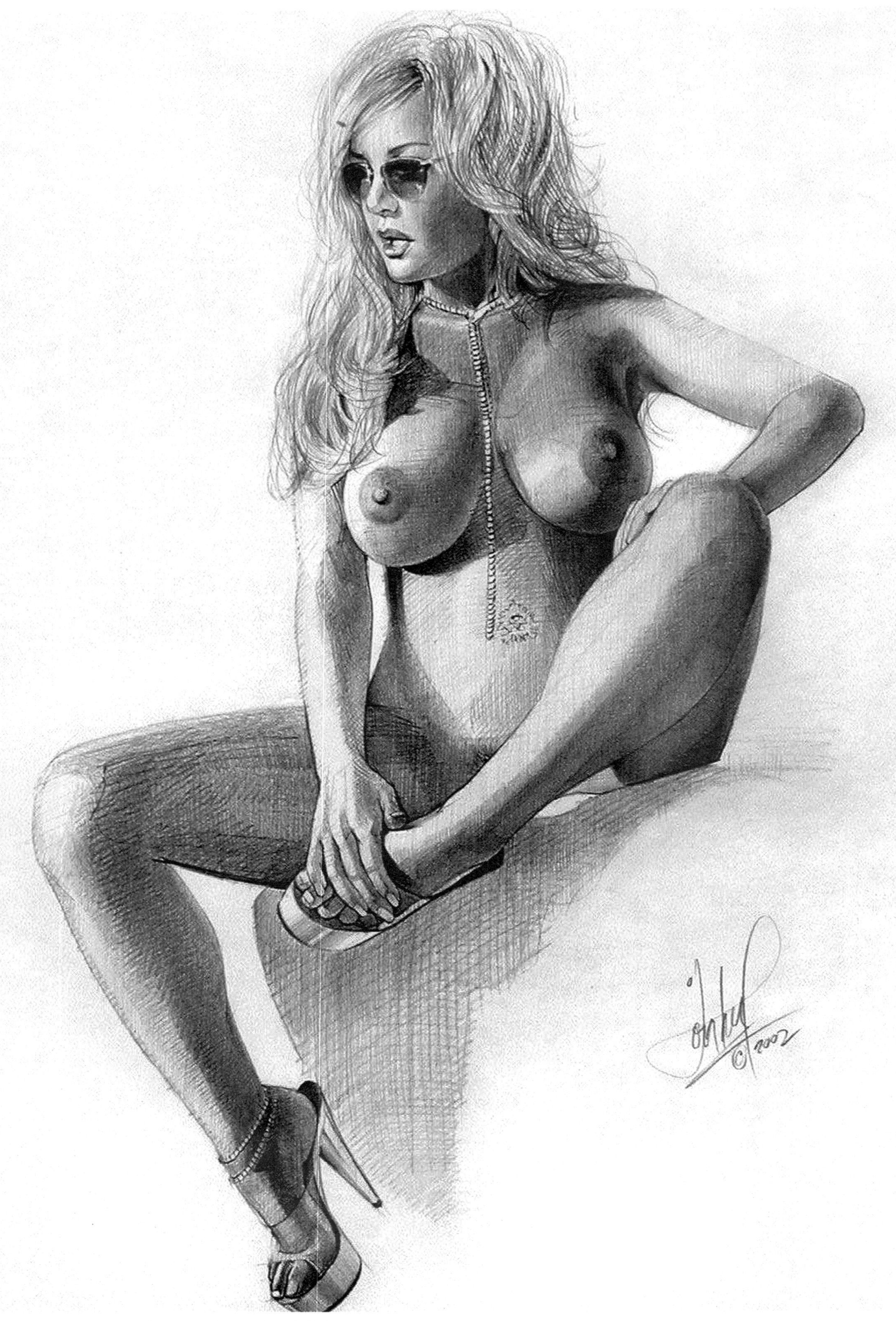